Life in a world of giants

How would you like living under subjection to eighteen-foot giants? As Dr. Narramore aptly notes, that's what it's like to be a little kid! If you have a young child up to seven years of age, you're probably two to three times his weight and considerably taller — a real giant!

Your Child's Hidden Needs is a real eye-opener. Perhaps for the first time since *you* were small you'll see things from a child's perspective. By wearing your child's emotional shoes, you'll become more aware of his deepest needs for confidence and self-esteem and learn how to deal with the power struggles that can lead to misbehavior.

Kids need a lot of confidence to live in a world of giants. Let *Your Child's Hidden Needs* help your child by helping you to approach him with sensitivity, encouragement, and praise.

Your Child's
HIDDEN
NEEDS

BY Bruce Narramore

Help! I'm a Parent
You're Someone Special
Freedom From Guilt (with Bill Counts)
No Condemnation
Adolescence Is Not an Illness
Cutting the Cord (with Vern Lewis)
Your Child's Hidden Needs

Your Child's
HIDDEN
NEEDS

Bruce Narramore

Power Books

Fleming H. Revell Company
Old Tappan, New Jersey

Unless otherwise identified, Scripture quotations in this book are from the Holy Bible, New International Version, copyright © 1973, 1978, 1984 International Bible Society. Used by permission of Zondervan Bible Publishers.

Scripture verses marked TLB are taken from The Living Bible, Copyright © 1971 by Tyndale House Publishers, Wheaton, Ill. Used by permission.

Scripture quotations identified NAS are from the New American Standard Bible, © The Lockman Foundation 1960, 1962, 1963, 1968, 1971, 1972, 1973, 1975, 1977.

Illustrations are taken from the book WHY CHILDREN MISBEHAVE by Bruce Narramore. Copyright © 1980 by the Zondervan Corporation, copyright © 1987 by Bruce Narramore. Used by permission of Zondervan Publishing House.

This book is a revised version of *Why Children Misbehave,* copyright © 1987 by Bruce Narramore, originally published by Zondervan Publishing House.

Illustrations by Diane Head

Library of Congress Cataloging-in-Publication Data

Narramore, Bruce.
    Your child's hidden needs / Bruce Narramore.
       p.   cm.
    Rev. version of: Why children misbehave. c1987.
    ISBN 0-8007-5337-2
    1. Parenting.   2. Child psychology.   I. Narramore, Bruce. Why children misbehave.   II. Title.
HQ755.8.N36   1990
649'.1—dc20   90-33098
                                               CIP

Copyright © 1980, 1981, 1987, 1990 by Bruce Narramore
Published by the Fleming H. Revell Company
Old Tappan, New Jersey 07675
Printed in the United States of America

Contents

Your Child's
HIDDEN
NEEDS

Part I
Parenting Can Be Positive

1

An Ounce of Prevention *Is* Worth a Pound of Cure!

Do you occasionally have "one of those days"? Shortly after you get up in the morning—or sometimes even before—things begin to fall apart. Something or somebody crashes to the floor in the kitchen. One of your children starts crying and the other gets into some kind of trouble. From that beginning, things get progressively worse. If you have young children, they are constantly fussing or whining about one thing or another. If you have teenagers, they've got the radio blaring all over the house. By the end of the day if you pause to reflect on what has happened, you probably decide that no two or three normal children could cause so much trouble unless they had stayed up late the night before plotting the whole thing!

If this happened only occasionally, most of us could cope fairly well. Unfortunately, many homes are like this every day. And most parents spend hours refereeing or policing their children's activities. We threaten, correct, or discipline

them. We drop what we are doing to settle a squabble or resolve a crisis. We keep reminding them to "say please," "clean your plate," or, "eat at least one bite of everything." We tell them to leave their sister alone, clean their rooms, take out the trash, or do their homework about a thousand times. Day after day we correct or discipline our children *after* they have gotten into trouble.

I call this a "fire engine approach" to parenting. We run

from one fire to another—but always *after* trouble has begun. Once in a while we step back long enough to vow to do better, but before long we are right back into our old patterns. Soon we feel so emotionally drained that we stop enjoying our children.

This doesn't have to be. There is another approach to parenting that focuses more on the fun times you can have with your children than it does on problems and misunderstandings. It focuses on positive parenting that nips problems in the bud rather than waiting for warfare to break out. And it focuses on increasing family unity and understanding instead of

constant nagging, bickering, and fighting. With a little practice you can help your family move toward a more enjoyable, upbeat family life together. You won't be able to eliminate all of your children's irritating attitudes and actions, but you will be able to avoid a lot of them. You can also learn to solve other problems before they reach serious proportions.

Several years ago I wrote *Help! I'm a Parent*[1] to show parents of young children some workable solutions to everyday discipline problems like mealtime hassles, temper tantrums, sibling fights, undone chores, and messy rooms. That book focuses largely on what to do after your children misbehave. This book is a companion to *Help! I'm a Parent* and focuses more on what to do before your children misbehave.

Your Child's Hidden Needs

Several years ago I had an experience that brought the importance of positive, preventive parenting forcefully home to me. I had been on the East Coast for a series of meetings. My plane arrived in Los Angeles around eight-thirty in the evening and by the time I got my baggage to the car and drove home it was nearly ten o'clock. Since I was still on Baltimore time, I felt more like it was 2:00 A.M. I was dog tired and looking forward to getting home and falling into bed.

I parked the car in the driveway, took out my briefcase and suitcase, and walked toward the house. Just as I reached for the doorknob I heard an awful crash and the yelling voices of my two young children. When I opened the door, there were Dickie and Debbie, both crying, on the floor with an overturned coffee table between them.

[1] Bruce Narramore, *Help! I'm a Parent*. Grand Rapids: Zondervan Publishing House, 1972.

I had had a long, hard day and didn't need this kind of a welcome. My first impulse was to yell, "What's the matter with you kids anyway? I just got home and you're already fighting!" I felt like telling them to "shut up, go to your rooms, and leave me alone!" It was past their bedtime anyway, and I was in no mood for this kind of hassle. Fortunately, I got my wits about me and thought, *What would you tell someone else to do in this kind of a mess?*

Then I realized what was going on. I had been away for a couple of days. Before that I had been extra busy at work. For nearly a week I hadn't had any quality time with the children. They both missed me and had been racing to the door to see which one could greet Daddy first. They were running, in other words, to get my love. But when I saw them in that pile, I'll have to admit I didn't recognize their need for love! Not until I stepped back and asked myself what was going on beneath the surface of my children's behavior could I understand the source of my disturbing welcome.

Once I realized what was going on, I sat down on the couch and said, "Dickie, come here." With a serious look on his face Dickie came over and sat down on my lap. I said, "Son, how would you like me to take you to school tomorrow morning? We could leave a few minutes early and go to McDonald's for breakfast on the way." Immediately Dickie brightened up. "Oh boy!" he exclaimed as he jumped up and headed on his way.

Then I called for Debbie. "Climb up here on my lap, honey," I said. And she did. "How about on Friday morning you and I go out for breakfast? Would you like to go to McDonald's, or would you rather go to Burger King?" "Burger King," Debbie immediately replied, since Dickie had chosen to go to McDonald's! And she was on her way.

I looked across the room and saw my wife with a threatening look in her eyes. "Honey," I said, "come sit on my lap." Then I asked her if she would like to go out to dinner the next evening!

After a few more minutes of family time, we put the children to bed and had our peace and quiet. The whole thing didn't take five or ten minutes but the atmosphere in our house went from complete chaos to real tranquility. All it took was for me to recognize the need for love that was hidden under Dickie and Debbie's fighting.

Learning to recognize your children's needs is the key to positive parenting. God created your children with several basic needs and put you in the best position to supply those needs. He created them with physical needs for food, shelter, and clothing. He created them with moral and spiritual needs. And He created them with social and emotional needs. Four of these emotional needs are especially important and the major focus of this book. For example, God created your children with a need for love. Your sons and daughters need to feel closely related to you and a few other significant people. They need to know that they are cared for and that they belong. They need to experience a "we" feeling and a sense of togetherness.

God also created your children with a need for feelings of confidence or competence. Children need to know that they have abilities and gifts they can use. They need to know they can master certain tasks and function competently at home and school and with their friends. Children also need to feel a sense of significance or worth. They need to know they are important and valuable to you and others. The needs for love, confidence, and worth are your children's deepest emotional needs. But God also created your children with a fourth related need. That is the need to be involved in interesting, enjoyable, constructive activities. When God placed Adam and Eve in the Garden of Eden, for example, He didn't tell them to sit down and stay out of His way. Instead, He immediately gave them a lot to do. They were to name the animals, multiply and replenish the earth, and rule over the earth under God's direction. In a similar fashion, your children need to have a variety of interesting and challenging activities to enjoy.

Why Children Misbehave

Your success in helping your children meet their God-given needs for love, confidence, worth, and constructive activity will impact their lives in two ways for years to come. First, as with Dickie and Debbie, your children's unmet emotional needs will push them toward a wide range of misbehaviors and create innumerable problems around the house. Anytime one of a child's needs isn't met, he will start looking for a substitute fulfillment. When children don't feel loved, for example, they turn to attention-getting misbehaviors. Since it's lonely to feel unloved, they misbehave to force you to drop what you are doing and spend a little time with them. In a similar way, when children lack confidence they can become stubborn and argumentative or try to lord it over their brothers and sisters in order to gain a temporary feeling of strength. And when they lack a sense of worth and value they may turn into driven, perfectionistic, or workaholic children in order to gain some positive feelings about themselves. Temper tantrums, sibling fights, bad attitudes, and periods of stubbornness can all grow out of the attempt to ward off feelings of being unloved, incompetent, unworthy, or bored by turning to a substitute or counterfeit fulfillment. We can illustrate this predictable sequence like this:

Figure 1

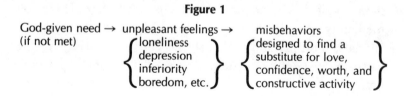

God-given need → unpleasant feelings →   misbehaviors
(if not met)   { loneliness   }   { designed to find a
                        depression   substitute for love,
                        inferiority   confidence, worth, and
                        boredom, etc. }   constructive activity }

Take temper tantrums, for example. Young children throw temper tantrums for one of two main reasons. First, they feel left out or ignored. They know you will come running and give them some attention if they throw a tantrum. Second, they throw tantrums when they feel weak or helpless or powerless. When they try to tie their shoelaces and can't, for example, they may cry and throw a tantrum. Or when they can't get their way with you, they throw a tantrum to force you to give in. They know if they cry long enough or loud enough you may eventually say, "Oh, all right!" and let them have their way. Their tantrum is a way of gaining some power or control over you.

Or consider sibling fights. We all know some children who are constantly picking at each other or teasing or engaging in physical combat. Sometimes these children have simply learned to argue from their parents. But more commonly, children fight because they feel incompetent, inferior, lonely, or bored. If you felt weak and inferior, wouldn't you feel bigger if you could beat up on your brother or sister? Or if you were feeling left out and unloved, wouldn't fighting with your brother get your parents' attention in a hurry? And what could you do if you were bored stiff and had no constructive activities to keep you busy? How about starting a fight with your little sister? That would eliminate boredom in a hurry! In similar ways, many of the daily hassles you have with your children grow out of their temporary feelings of being unloved, incompetent, unworthy, or bored.

Roots of Self-Esteem

Your children's needs for love, confidence, and worth also form the building blocks of their developing self-esteem. Children who grow up feeling loved, confident, and worthy, tend to feel good about themselves and others. They know they are lovable and that they have abilities and are significant individuals. This enables them to get along well with others, to have the confidence to try new things, and to accept new challenges. When hard times hit, people with good self-concepts may become temporarily discouraged or downhearted, but they don't cave in like people who fundamentally do not believe they are worth much or have many abilities.

Children whose needs for love, confidence, and worth are not well met can be especially susceptible to painful feelings of failure, depression, and anxiety. Throughout their lives they may approach new situations with the expectation that they will not be liked or that they will fail. Even after years of outward success, many adults who grew up doubting their abilities still question the adequacy of their performance or their basic sense of significance or value. Others shackle their spontaneity for fear of making mistakes or being rejected. Still others drive themselves unmercifully toward some perfectionistic goal or standard which they mistakenly believe will finally provide some self-acceptance.

Actions Speak Louder Than Words

Unfortunately, most children aren't very good at articulating their needs and letting their parents see them clearly. Like Dickie and Debbie fighting to be the first to meet me at the door, few young children can quietly greet their father and, after a few pleasantries, say, "Dad, we have been feeling a little lonely lately. You have been gone so much, we are afraid you think your work is more important than us. Do you think we could find some time alone together so we could feel more loved and special to you?" Instead, they run to the door, fight, or keep interrupting us in a vain attempt to get us to see how they really feel inside.

Few teenagers, even when they are very depressed, are able to say, "Mom [or Dad], I'm lonely and depressed and need your help. I don't know what's the matter, but I just need you." Instead, they keep their sadness to themselves, become angry, sullen, and hard to live with, or they seek relief through alcohol, drugs, or sex.

This creates a major problem for parents. Since our children generally don't clearly express their needs, we have to learn to see the hidden needs that lie beneath their actions. That's the major focus of this book. In coming chapters we will look at each of your children's four God-given needs, see how you can recognize and help your children meet them, and demonstrate what happens if you don't.

Chapter Highlights

Although children need discipline and correction after they misbehave, many potential problems can be prevented and many others quickly solved when we learn to recognize our children's hidden needs. Every child has four important God-given emotional needs. They need to feel loved, confident, and worthy, and they need to be involved in interesting activities. These needs are the key to many of your children's misbehaviors and to their future life's adjustment. Before we look more closely at these needs, we want to look at one other reason children act and feel the way they do. That's the topic of chapter 2.

2
Your Child *Is* Different!

If you have more than one child, the chances are they were different from each other since the day you brought them home from the hospital. One may have been a peaceful child who fit nicely into your arms, enjoyed being held, and soon fell into a happy routine of eating and sleeping. He was happy, easy to please, and showed a good bit of flexibility.

Your next child was probably very different. Right from the start he was more active and fidgety. He didn't fit quite as comfortably into your arms, and his eating and sleeping patterns were fussy and erratic. While your first child could sleep through an earthquake, you couldn't tiptoe into the second one's room without waking him up. Little things upset him. He was more active than his brother. He wore his feelings on his sleeve. He experienced things strongly, and he wanted what he wanted right now!

No matter how similarly you treat these children, they are

bound to be different as they're growing up. And no matter how perfect a parent you may be, there is every likelihood that you will have more struggles with the second child because his basic personality is different.

Some years ago two child psychiatrists, Alexander Thomas and Stella Chess, completed a twenty-year study of the temperament and development of a large number of children from infancy through adolescence.[1] The children were studied in order to determine the effect of temperament on personality development and to see how children's basic temperaments interact with their environment to shape their later life adjustment. After rating each child on nine different dimensions of temperament, the researchers were able to group the children into three general categories.[2] One group was labeled "the Easy Child," another "the Slow-to-Warm-Up Child," and the third, "the Difficult Child." Thomas and Chess found that even though children in each group changed, they tended to retain the same general personality style throughout their growing years.

The Easy Child

"Easy Children" tend to adapt well to new situations, develop regular eating and sleeping schedules, be rather predictable and consistent, meet new people with a smile, and handle frustration rather well. They are adaptable rather than demanding, and because they are not high-strung, their par-

[1] Alexander Thomas and Stella Chess, *Temperament and Development* (New York: Brunner-Mazel, 1977).
[2] The nine dimensions were activity level, rhythmicity, approach or withdrawal, adaptability, threshold of responsiveness, intensity of reaction, quality of mood, distractibility and attention span, and persistence.

ents are able to relax and take life easier. Parents of these children feel less need to threaten, pressure, or worry, and since we worry less, we feel better about ourselves and our roles as parents. In fact, if all of your children were Easy Children you probably wouldn't need to read a book on parenting!

The Slow-to-Warm-Up Child

The second type of child Chess and Thomas discovered was the "Slow-to-Warm-Up Child." Children in this group tend to have a mildly negative response to anything or anyone new. In contrast to Easy Children, Slow-to-Warm-Up Children meet strangers with hesitancy or mild negativism. If you take them to a new social setting, they don't enter in quickly. If you take them to a new church nursery, instead of walking confidently into their new surroundings, they cling to your skirt or pants. They may even cry a little and plead, "Don't go." But once you leave, they gradually warm up, and by the time you return to pick them up, they are probably having a fine time.

Slow-to-Warm-Up Children also tend to approach new foods, new activities, and new experiences hesitantly. Their first response to new food is, "No." And their first response to new people is rather quiet and guarded. But if they are handled

carefully, they gradually warm up and learn to relate well. They just take a little time.

The Difficult Child

The third type of child is called the "Difficult Child." Children in this group are almost the exact opposite of the Easy Children. They are irregular and unpredictable, they have intense, often negative moods, their eating and sleeping habits are irregular, and they frequently laugh or cry loudly. Children like this can be difficult to parent. They don't tend to draw warm, fuzzy responses from parents because they don't fit nicely into the family routine. They don't charm strangers at the market the way Easy Children do. And they don't even take the quiet, hesitant approach of Slow-to-Warm-Up Children. Instead, Difficult Children make their presence known in ways that can be upsetting. They cry, fuss, fight, and in scores of ways refuse to adapt.

Difficult Children tend to stir up anger and frustration in their parents. We become irritated because they "won't cooperate" or because they upset our routine and make our lives difficult. They can also provoke a lot of parental anxiety and guilt since we assume we are somehow to blame for their maladaptive style.

To Each His Own

You don't have to be a psychologist to realize that these
three types of children call for
very different skills and sensitivities on the part of parents.
What is good for one of these
children will not necessarily be
good for the other. Easy Children can end up having problems just because they are so
easy. Placed in a family with a
Difficult Child, Easy Children
can be lost in the cracks. Their
more aggressive, active, or
negativistic brothers and sisters are more likely to become

the center of attention because their antics stir greater parental concern. Consequently parents of Easy Children have to
be especially sensitive to their needs for encouragement, attention, and support.

Slow-to-Warm-Up Children need parents who neither neglect their needs to learn to adapt to new situations nor push
them into situations before they are ready. Sensitive parents
offer Slow-to-Warm-Up Children new opportunities and gen-
tly encourage them, but they do not pressure. They also avoid
holding out a model of a socially gregarious child before the
Slow-to-Warm-Up.

My wife and I had to learn this with our son. For the first
eight years or so of his life, Dickie was rather shy and not too
sociable. Every time company came over, my wife encour-

aged Dickie to be more sociable. She repeatedly told him, "Speak up," "Look them in the eyes," or, "Don't act so disinterested." Although I wasn't as worried about Dickie's quiet style (since I am that way myself), I soon started trying to help Kathy get Dickie to become more outgoing. After a few months of this we finally realized what we were doing. We were subtly telling Dickie, "We don't like you the way you are. You should be more outgoing like your sister." Realizing this could undercut his positive feelings about himself, we began to remove the pressure. We focused more on having good times with Dickie, encouraging him to bring friends home from school and getting him involved in athletics and other activities. Gradually, he become more outgoing and socially alert, but not because we pressured him. Dickie will probably never be the clown or life of the party, but he is now a very sociable and delightful young man.

Parents of Difficult Children have to be careful not to be drawn into a cycle of negativism. Instead of responding to their good, cooperative moments, it's easy to wait until things go wrong and then correct them. Unfortunately, this reinforces their difficult style and encourages them to think of themselves as "bad" or "problem children." If you can help Difficult Children channel their energy in constructive ways, they can be very successful, creative individuals. But if you focus only on their "difficulties" they can live up to your worst expectations. Difficult Children need reasonable and consistent limits and they need to be kept constructively occupied in order to maximize their best potential.

When Thomas and Chess analyzed their data on the three temperament types, they attempted to find out which group had the most behavior problems. Much to many parents' surprise, it wasn't the Difficult Children. Neither was it the

Slow-to-Warm-Up Children. It wasn't even the Easy Children. Thomas and Chess found that no one temperamental group had any more problems than the others. There were well-adjusted and problem children in each group. When any of the children had problems, however, they were caused by a combination of the child's temperament and the family or school environment. Many Difficult Children, for example, got along great because their parents were not easily upset by their active, often impulsive style. They were able to set limits carefully and sensitively. Other parents with the same type of children were unable to control them and suffered immense guilt and frustration as a result.

The same was true of the Slow-to-Warm-Up and Easy Children. When parents of Slow-to-Warm-Up kids were sensitive to their unique needs and characteristics, the children did well. It was only when the parents of Slow-to-Warm-Up Children had trouble adapting to their children's style that they had problems. The key to the children's adjustment was found in how well the children's and the parents' styles "fit" each other. That is, were the parents able to tune in to their children's style, appreciate it, and learn to cope in a positive, accepting, and consistent manner? To put this another way, it is possible to have an Easy Child but to be a "difficult" parent!

A Proverb for Parents

Centuries before psychologists started studying these differences between children, the Bible made the very same point. Proverbs 22:6 says, "Train a child in the way he should go, and when he is old he will not turn from it." Some parents have assumed this verse means that we should take our children to Sunday school and church, see that they avoid certain sinful activities, and engage in selected disciplines like Bible study and prayer. Then, in spite of the training, they may pass through a period of rebellion during adolescence or young adulthood, but sometime in their later years will return to God.

Actually, though, the phrase "in the way he should go" does not refer at all to some prescribed path cut out for every person to follow regardless of his or her individuality. The word *way* is used in chapter 30 of Proverbs to refer to "the way of an eagle in the sky, the way of a snake on a rock, the way of a ship on the high seas, and the way of a man with a maiden" (vv. 18, 19). In every case "the way" refers to a unique, spontaneous direction or style. One theologian put it like this: " 'The way' can have no other meaning than 'according to the standard of his way' . . . in the sense of his own natural and characteristic style and manner and then his training will have reference to that to which he is naturally filled."[3] In other words, as parents we need to seek out our children's strengths, abilities, and potential, and help them move in the direction in which they point.

We should not take a Slow-to-Warm-Up Child and try to turn him into an outgoing, life-of-the-party, social butterfly. We should not try to transform an Easy Child into a loud, aggressive person. And we should not try to make a Difficult Child become a quiet, prim and proper person. With age, positive parenting, and broadened experience, all of these children may move a bit in the direction we would like. But our goal should be to find their style and help them channel it

---

[3] J. P. Lange, ed, *Lange's Commentary on the Holy Scriptures*, 12 vols. (Grand Rapids: Zondervan Publishing House, 1960), 5:192.

in positive directions. If they need some rough edges smoothed out, so be it, but we must always respect their basic God-given temperaments or styles.

Sometimes one parent has difficulty relating to a child because his temperament is so totally different from the parent's that he cannot even comprehend it. A friend of mine, for example, is a real "Southern lady." She is an outstanding person, extremely well-mannered, sensitive, and socially alert. She knows just how to react in every social situation and wants her children to do the same. Unfortunately, one of her children has a very different temperament. As an adolescent, the girl couldn't care less about some of her mother's most cherished social values. At times she doesn't even *want* to be polite! This practically drives her mother crazy and is the source of repeated conflict. Fortunately the girl's father is more like his daughter and can help his wife moderate her tendency to try to turn her daughter into something that she isn't.

Other parents clash with one of their children simply because they *are* so much alike. One high-strung, anxious person in the family is plenty. To have a child with the same temperament is just too much! Two easily frustrated and somewhat impulsive people can have serious conflicts.

If you find yourself clashing with one of your children, you can take two steps to minimize the problem. First, be sure to let your spouse play an active role in the training. Your husband or wife is probably different from you and can help you understand what your child is thinking or feeling. Second, search out why your child is triggering your negative responses. Does he remind you of yourself when you were a child? Is he like a brother you fought for years? Is he too much like your husband or wife? Or is he exactly the type of child you swore you would never rear? Whatever the reason, once you understand why that child pushes your button, you should be able to be more sensitive and patient.

Why Are Children So Different?

Inborn temperaments aren't the only reason children can be so different. There is one more important determinant of your children's personality uniqueness. That is his or her place in the family constellation.

First children have both advantages and disadvantages. First children are often the most cherished. They are mother's first baby, and this evokes some strong positive feelings from her. At the same time, mothers of first children have had no previous practice. They tend to worry excessively over little details and take incessant care of their "precious little one." This anxious caring can make it difficult for first children to reach out on their own, try new things, and learn to handle their hurts. Situations that arouse great concern in mothers of first children are often ignored by the time the second or third child comes along, and this more relaxed attitude can really help a child.

When second children enter the family, older children encounter more pains and pleasures. As older children, they probably have more freedom, more responsibilities, and more opportunities to do as they please. Their new brothers or sisters, however, have replaced them as the baby of the family. The helpless new infants, no matter how wonderful they may be, now have more of mother's time and attention. This can make older children feel displaced and rejected, and often stirs feelings of resentment toward the new sibling.

As children grow, younger children discover there are both advantages and disadvantages to being second in line. As the baby, they often get by with murder. They can provoke their older siblings, cry, and see their brother or sister become the object of mother's wrath. They quickly find all the advantages of being the baby and learn to use them well! At the same time, younger children know that their older siblings have more freedom. Older brothers and sisters get to stay up later and play outside longer, for example. This makes younger children feel a bit inferior or resentful.

If a third child comes along, everything shifts again. From the position of being the baby, second children now become the "sandwich child." They are sandwiched in between their older brother or sister (who has all the freedoms and privileges of the eldest) and the baby (who has all the advantages of being the baby). If you aren't careful, middle children can become lost in the shuffle. They don't have the advantages of either the oldest or the youngest child.

With the arrival of a third child, eldest children are pushed still further from mother. They may respond with feelings of isolation or rejection, which they try to cover by asserting

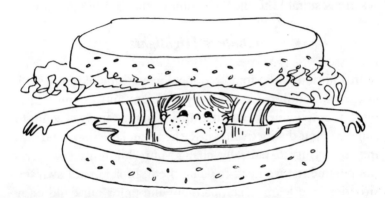

themselves physically over one of their younger siblings. If they can't gain their identity by being close to Mother, they might be able to do it by dominating a brother or sister. Eldest children can also take advantage of their position as the most mature. In receiving a larger allowance, staying out longer, staying up later, and in general having more freedom, they gain some positive feelings.

Third children, of course, now hold the position of the baby. What they can't gain through strength, age, and competition, they can gain by being the baby. So, just as the second child may have done earlier, third children can make full use of their helplessness to try to gain their way as much as possible. Sometimes first or second children sense the advantages of being a baby and go through a brief period of regression in which they become more babylike. They regress back to baby talk, become more tearful or helpless, and may even lose some of their toilet control for a few weeks after a new baby comes into the home.

These feelings and reactions are only a few of many possibilities. Not every child reacts in a typical or expected manner, yet most children do express some rather predictable reactions suitable to their position in the family structure.

Chapter Highlights

In addition to the four emotional needs all children have in common, children are also very different and unique. Their inborn temperaments and their place in the family account for some of their distinctiveness. Rather than labeling, condemning, or trying to radically change our children's God-given temperaments, we need to value them, broaden our own sensitivities, and learn to complement and enjoy our children no matter how different or difficult they seem to be. In other words, we must learn the best ways to help each child feel loved, confident, and worthy, and we must find the best ways to keep them actively involved in constructive activities. The way we do that will vary from child to child.

The rest of this book focuses on the four universal human needs and some principles of parenting that apply to every child. Before we move on to these needs, however, let's summarize the important principles of parenting that grow out of our understanding of our children's individual differences.

1. Because of their unique physiological makeup and position in the family, all children will have somewhat different temperaments and personalities.

2. Children's temperaments vary widely within a normal range, and there is no one "right" temperament.

3. Since many of our children's reaction tendencies are inborn, we should not blame ourselves for these differences in style.

4. It is always best to flow with our children's basic direction or style rather than to push them into some opposite style.

5. Since children are different from one another, we must treat them differently if we are to treat them fairly. We will need to be flexible in our training and correction so we can meet the needs of all our children.

6. Given sensitive parenting, children with vastly different styles can grow up to be healthy, happy, and productive adults. The differences between styles enrich the world and bring stimulating experiences.

7. Children may have unique struggles or feelings because of their position in the family.

8. With good family experiences, time, and other relationships, our children's temperaments tend to mature
   and the rough edges are rounded off.

With these background understandings, let's turn to the
first of your children's four basic God-given emotional needs,
the need for love.

Part II
Your Child's
Hidden Needs

3
Mommy, Do You Love Me?

Have you ever been preparing a meal for company or involved in some other task when your daughter walked in and asked, "Mommy, will you play with me?" If you are like most of us, the chances are you replied, "I'm sorry, sweetheart, but Mommy's busy right now." Somewhat disappointed, your daughter turned away and busied herself for the next few minutes. Soon she was back again. "Mommy [or Daddy]," she asked with a bit more urgency, "will you play with me *now?*" "Honey," you replied with growing frustration in your voice, "can't you see I'm busy?" Once again your child trudged off, this time obviously unhappy. She felt left out and like a second-class person compared with the company you had on your mind.

You returned to work, but after a while you realized it had been quiet a little too long so you decided to investigate. Sure enough, as you started down the hall, you detected the aroma of your most expensive perfume, or you saw some beautiful

artistic creation on the wall, or you found the end of the roll
of toilet paper yards from its original source. When you tracked
it down, you were amazed at how many feet of paper there are
in one small roll! If you have more than one child, instead of
thirty minutes of "dangerous silence," your rebuffed daughter may simply go to the other end of the house and start
hassling her sister. Before long, they are on the verge of war.

What were your daughter's actions telling you? Wasn't she
saying, "Mother [or Dad], if you won't show me you love me
and want to be with me when I am being good, then I will get
into trouble to force you to give me your attention"? Anytime

children feel lonely, isolated, or left out, they tend to turn to some type of attention-getting misbehavior. They know that if they cause enough commotion, their parents will come running. What parent can ignore a budding Rembrandt who has chosen the living room wall as his canvas? What parent can ignore two screaming children engaged in hand-to-hand combat? And what parent can ignore a teenager who is on drugs, breaking curfew, or failing Sophomore English? Figure 2 illustrates this predictable series of events: First, the young girl has a God-given need for love. Next, her parents are too busy to help her meet that need so she feels isolated and alone. Finally, since she can't get rid of her bad feelings by being good, she misbehaves to gain her parents' attention as a temporary substitute for love and the sense of belonging.

Let me ask you a frank question: When would you say you give your children your most complete attention? When do

Figure 2

God-Given Need:	When Need Is Not Met:	Child Turns to Substitute of:
Love	Loneliness and Isolation	Attention

you lay everything else aside and focus totally on your sons and daughters? Is it when they are well-mannered, cooperative, and constructively occupying themselves? Or is it when they have interrupted your activities with fussing, fighting, or crying?

If you are like most parents, you will probably have to admit that you give your children your fullest attention when they misbehave. As long as they are happily busying themselves in front of the television, in their own rooms, or with a friend, most of us go about our work and pay limited attention to our children. We may even think, *Great, they are busy. Now's my chance to get some work done!* But as soon as our sons and daughters misbehave, we drop whatever we are doing, run to them, look them in the eye, and give them our undivided attention. But consider what we have done: We have neglected their needs when they were behaving well and attended to their needs when they misbehaved. In effect we were teaching them to misbehave if they wanted our time and attention!

Love Is Not Enough

Bill and Connie dearly loved their fifteen-year-old daughter, Kristen. They both worked to provide a nice home for their family, took Kristen to one school or church activity after another, and provided extremely well for her physical and financial needs. They were also concerned about Kristen's values and her friends and they supported her activities at school where Kristen was a solid B student. They were completely shocked to return from work one day and find Kristen unconscious on her bedroom floor from an overdose of drugs.

Fortunately, they got their daughter to a hospital in time and Kristen's life was spared. Later, in my office, Kristen told me, "I guess my parents love me, but it doesn't do me any good. Mom and I are always fighting. I know she does a lot for me, but she's always on my case. She doesn't like my friends. She complains about my room. And she keeps telling me how lazy or unhelpful I am around the house. I wouldn't mind helping if she showed a little appreciation, but I just feel like I'm a bother. I can't tell my mom how I feel because she'd just criticize me more or tell me to stop feeling sorry for myself. All Dad does is tell me to stop arguing with Mom or be more helpful around the house."

Although Bill and Connie loved their daughter very much, their love wasn't soaking in. There was a big gap between their love for Kristen and their ability to express it in ways that she could understand it and receive it. Their busy schedules, inability to relax and have fun with their daughter, and their tendency to criticize and accuse Kristen of being lazy and unhelpful made her feel terribly alone and misunderstood. Even though she knew in her head that her parents cared for her, that knowledge wasn't helping her with her daily feelings.

Like Kristen, many children feel very lonely, discouraged, and unappreciated. A lot of this isn't their parents' fault. Teenagers tend to have a difficult time of life. They struggle with their physical looks, their changing minds and bodies, and acceptance by their peers. But we parents can unknowingly complicate their problems. Since teenagers are already so prone to feel rejected and inferior, they are extremely vulnerable to any parental criticism or pressuring. Children, and especially teenagers, frequently interpret our comments and actions quite differently than we intend. *We* think, *I'm working hard to take care of my family. They* think, *Mom and Dad are so busy doing their own thing they don't care about us. We* think, *I want to help her be responsible. They* think, *She doesn't like me. All she ever does is criticize.* And *we* think, *Boy, I'm tired. I think I'll turn on the TV and relax.* But *they* think, *There he goes again. He really doesn't care.*

If you want to rear healthy, happy children, you must understand this fact: It is not enough to love your children. It isn't even enough to devote your life to see that they have fine clothes, a nice vacation, and a good education. No matter how deeply you love your children, your love is of little value until your children experience it in ways that let them take it in and receive it and believe it. Psychologists' offices are filled with people whose parents loved them. But for a variety of reasons they weren't able to experience their parents' love and let it reach deep into their lives.

Like Bill and Connie's, many parents' love doesn't soak in. Children have small emotional "fuel tanks" and they need frequent "fill ups" to be reminded of how loved they are. They need us to look them directly in the eye and pay attention to them in the morning. They need us to send them off to school with a hug and a warm good-bye. They need us to greet them when they come home from school. They need us to show an interest in their day's activities and their thoughts and feelings. They need to play and have fun with us. And they need to be told they're loved and shown it physically. Only a steady dose of love expressed in many ways can fill up a child's emotional fuel tank and convince him he is loved no matter what.

Many teenage girls become excessively boy-crazy because they are looking for a substitute for the love they don't feel at home. One mother, reflecting on her own teenage years, told me, "The most difficult struggle I had was not being able to communicate with my father. I wanted to be close and comfortable with him, but he was awkward about showing his love for me. I became boy-crazy at fourteen and realized a loved feeling from a man for my first time. From then on, I lived from one date to the next. I carried this vacuum into my marriage. I deeply want to be loved, but I have trouble accepting it when it's there."

Other children respond in just the opposite way; steeling themselves against intimacy, they put up a front and act as though they really don't need love. Unfortunately, this cuts them off from deep, enriching relationships and leaves them feeling sterile, empty, and angry inside.

When I speak of children feeling unloved, I don't necessarily mean your children are walking around reflecting on how lonely and unloved they are, or contemplating some drastic action like suicide. More often, children simply feel like they are a bother to someone, or they feel left out, or alone. Loneliness can show itself in depression, in the feeling of not being understood, in angry rebellion, or in disruptive attention-getting behavior.

Communicating Love to Children

During the seventies and eighties an interesting phrase became popular with many parents and educators: It's not the *quantity* of time you spend with your children, they claimed, it's the *quality* that matters. With the rapid increase in working mothers and two-career families, parents realized they were spending less and less time with their children. They also started feeling guilty, so they decided, "It's quality, not quantity." To a degree this is true. All the time in the world is useless if we simply use it to berate or pressure or criticize our children. And a little quality time is better than a lot of anxious, angry, or conflicted time. But this is only one part of the story. Children need both quality and quantity.

Quality time means more than watching the same television program or being in the same house together. It includes focused time when children really feel our caring presence. It includes playing together, laughing together, and sharing intimate, loving moments. Infants see love in our adoring looks. Toddlers see it in the pleasure in our eyes as they excitedly show us their discoveries. School-age children see it when we listen to their hurts and when we play and share together. And adolescents feel our love when we support them, listen to their day's activities, and take pleasure in their accomplishments and activities. But even the best of these moments lose much of their effectiveness when they are few and far between.

Even loving parents can fall into a busy routine that unknowingly robs their families of times of real togetherness and love. Most of us have to work and we come home tired. Most of us attend church or are involved in various community activities. We also have friends, hobbies, and other responsibilities and needs. Even the time we spend doing things *for* our children can interfere with our time to be *with* them. We are busy chauffeuring one child to school, another to soccer, and a third to another school event or a church activity. The only other times our paths cross is at mealtimes or briefly on the way to church. And those are usually not the quietest, richest times of life!

At mealtimes we may be cajoling our children to eat their vegetables or mind their manners, and on Sunday mornings we are probably whirling through the house trying to get everyone out the door on time. There is nothing inherently wrong with doing so many things for our children. In fact, most children appreciate our frantic efforts. But if we don't watch it, we can get so busy doing things for our children that we fail to have any loving, quiet, or fun moments together. Your children don't just need a taxi driver, a chef, an organizer, a maid, and a disciplinarian. They also need parents who enjoy them and have meaningful, fun times with them. Those times, much more than all you do for them, communicate a deep sense of belonging and a feeling of being loved and understood.

Several years ago my wife and I had to face this fact. We loved our children dearly and wanted the best for them but Kathy and I are also active, busy people. We didn't want to wake up twenty years later and say, "What happened? We loved our children. What went wrong?"

To avoid that, we took a close look at our family's life-style. We realized that I often came home feeling too tired to play with the children. Kathy was so busy entertaining or leading study groups that she also found it difficult to give the children as much time as they needed. So we decided to rearrange our schedules to put our children first. The first thing Kathy did was to cancel a seminar she was about to teach on parenting. She decided it was more important to meet our children's needs than to teach other mothers how to be better parents!

I decided to find some way to relax and unwind at the end of a day so I could be available to do some fun things with Dickie and Debbie. For me that didn't come easy. I grew up on a farm in Arizona where there was not much playtime. My father would get up early to feed the cattle or do other chores before breakfast. Then he would put in ten or twelve more hours of work. After school and in the summers, my brother and I were expected to do our share. Although we had plenty of opportunities to play alone or with each other, we didn't share a lot of opportunities to relax and play with Dad. He was tired after a full day's work and didn't feel like throwing around a football, working on a jigsaw puzzle, or playing the latest fad game. The closest I got to Dad was to pull off his heavy work shoes as he lay in his easy chair reading the evening paper after a long day's work.

When I became a parent, I began to follow my dad's example. Being a confirmed workaholic, I found it difficult to spend relaxed time with our children. I could find a little time to teach them or offer some advice but I wasn't good at having fun together. Since I knew Dickie and Debbie needed me, I made a commitment to try to change my ways. I began by deciding to cut out a few extraneous activities, leave some work at the office, and spend at least half an hour with Dickie and Debbie every day. About that time, some friends told us about Lego blocks, those small indestructible building blocks for kids.

Dickie and I went downtown and bought our first batch of Lego blocks. We started with your basic log cabin kind of house—four walls, a roof, and a door. But as our architectural skills improved, we became more daring. We built larger houses. We built a fire station. And we built a battery-powered train that would actually run on a small track. At first I felt a little awkward getting on the floor and playing blocks with my children. *After all,* I thought, *I'm a psychologist with a Ph.D. I work in a think factory. Isn't this a little beneath my dignity?* But I soon realized I was enjoying playing with the blocks. In fact, I found playing blocks with my children helped me relax and unwind better at the end of a hard day's work than I could watching the six o'clock news or reading the newspaper to see what new disaster was occurring.

Over a period of a year or so I increasingly learned to enjoy my children. One night a week Kathy fixed whatever the children wanted for supper. Then we cleared the table and spent an hour or so playing games together. As the children got older I occasionally left work early to go to their three o'clock athletic events. Little by little I learned to relax and enjoy being with my family. But this didn't happen by chance. I had to work at it.

If you are like me, you too may need to sit down and make a list of your priorities. Write out the most important things in life to you. Mate, children, and relationship with God are high on most parents' priority lists. Then make a chart showing the way you actually spend your time. List the amount of time you spend sleeping, working, watching television, in social activities, at church, in the car, and anywhere else that is a familiar scene in your life. Then list the amount of time you spend daily with your sons and daughters talking, playing, or in some way sharing together.

If you are like most parents, you will find that some of the things at the top of your list of priorities are near the bottom of the chart that reflects the way you actually spend your time. One of the most life-changing decisions your family can make is to sit down with that list and rearrange your schedule so that you can spend more time on what you really value and less on other things.

Of course there are some practical limitations to rearranging schedules. You can't quit your job and stay home all day with your children. You also need some time alone and with your spouse and friends. And you probably have a number of survival tasks like cooking, cleaning, and yard work that must be done. But most of us spend more time in unessential activities than necessary. We lose time through poor planning and preparation. And we spend a lot of time in activities that, while fine in themselves, force us to minimize or neglect more important activities.

If you need help getting started, make a commitment to a friend to spend a minimum of fifteen to thirty minutes a day being *with* your children. The activity isn't important as long as it's something you both enjoy. If you can't find something you both enjoy, begin with something your children want to do. In time your tastes may change and their interests will mature.

The Television Trap

In our home television was one of those "okay" activities that started interfering with our life together. I am the kind of person who will flip on the TV just to see whether anything good is on. When our children were young I always watched the ten o'clock news, Monday evening football, and a few other programs. Dickie and Debbie also spent a great deal of time watching the TV. We didn't realize we had a problem until our television set went on the blink. Since we didn't have much money, we decided not to repair it for a while. Much to our surprise, we soon noticed a change in our family atmosphere. Within a couple of weeks Kathy and I were communicating more. We were spending more time with the children, and in general we were experiencing more "togetherness." Since things were going so well we decided to forget the television and continue enjoying our times together.

A year or so later we felt we had matured enough to control our television rather than letting it control us. So we went to

K mart and invested $100 in a small portable set. But before long we were right back into our old habits. I was back to the news and football; the kids were back to their programs. We were having fewer fun times together and our time was starting to revolve around the television set again, so we made a difficult decision. We called Goodwill Industries and asked them to take the set off our hands!

Our children weren't in school yet and we didn't get another television set until they both left home for college. I am convinced we had many more fun times together as a family than we would if we had kept the television. I'm also sure our children didn't feel deprived. In fact, several years ago we were returning from vacation and Dickie (then eight) was reading a newspaper. All of a sudden he exclaimed, "Hey, Dad, look at this!" Then he read me a brief article that said ninety-nine out of every one hundred homes in the United States have at least one television. After reading the item, he said with a bit of pride, "Gee, Dad, we're in the one percent!" He took pride in knowing we were not like everyone else. On a couple of occasions, I overheard our children explaining to their friends that we didn't have a television because "we like to do fun things together as a family!" I am also convinced this is one reason our children are avid readers and did well in school.

Please don't misunderstand me. I don't think television is inherently bad. We occasionally watched TV at a friend's home or visited grandmother in order to see a certain program. It seems to me, however, that even good programs can become a habit that reaches almost to the point of addiction. In fact, one group of researchers in Detroit offered 120 families $500 to do without television for one month's time, and 93 of the families refused the offer! They didn't believe it was worth $500 to give up television for one month.

Personally, I find that hard to believe. It seems to me they could at least have taken the $500, abstained for thirty days, and then used the money to purchase a new color set! But apparently the addiction was too strong. And the twenty-seven families who accepted the offer had some very unusual experiences. Nearly all of them initially reported periods of boredom, nervousness, and depression. They were so unaccustomed to entertaining themselves that at first they didn't know what to do.

Another study found that nearly half of the twelve-year-olds they surveyed watch television for an average of six or more hours each day. Dividing TV watchers into light watchers (two hours or less daily) and heavy watchers (four or more hours daily), the researchers discovered that heavy watchers were more likely to view the real world as dangerous and violent than were the light watchers. The researchers concluded that a heavy diet of television violence instilled fear in heavy viewers and caused them to be significantly more distrustful of other people and to overestimate their chances of being the victim of violence.

My prime concern, however, is not to stress the possible negative influences of television. There are many good programs for both children and adults. When viewed selectively, television can be a positive influence and an effective educational instrument. I am simply suggesting that television is one of the forces in our culture that can subtly split families apart and keep us from taking time to enjoy some truly uplifting and constructive times together. Active participation in family activities is much more enriching and ultimately rewarding than being passively entertained by the tube.

Some friends of ours have come up with a less drastic solution to the television problem than total abstinence. They
purchase *TV Guide* every Saturday, sit down as a family, and
decide what programs they will watch during the next week.
They impose a limit of about an hour each day, and the
programs must be selected ahead of time. This allows them to
choose good programs and averts the possibility of just click-
ing on the tube when they don't know what else to do. Other
families limit their viewing carefully and then spend time
discussing the issues and perspectives raised by the programs.

These solutions are probably better than ours, but if you are a potential "televisionholic" you may need our more drastic solution.

Chapter Highlights

Your children's most basic emotional need is to be loved and know that they belong. When children don't feel loved, they either turn to misbehaviors to gain attention or start feeling they are unlovable. Unfortunately, loving your children is not enough. Your sons and daughters have small emotional fuel tanks and need repeated, daily refills. To make sure your love is soaking in, periodically step back and take stock of your priorities. Be sure you are spending quality time with your sons and daughters and enjoying them. Look them in the eye. Pay attention to their conversation. Play with them. Let them know when you will be home and give them times to count on being together. Children receive your love in different ways at different ages, but they always need tangible expressions of your caring for them and their importance in your family.

4
Living in a World of Giants

If you have a child younger than six or seven years of age you are probably two or three times his size. He may weigh forty or fifty pounds, but you probably weigh between one and two hundred. You are also a great deal taller. To see things from your child's perspective, let's imagine that two people are assigned to you who are three times your size. They are each eighteen feet tall and weigh five hundred pounds. These giants follow you everywhere you go. They repeatedly tell you, "Hurry up," "Slow down," "Speak up," and "Quiet down." One of these giants cooks your food; the other one makes you eat it. You call one of them Mother and the other Father. Everywhere you go, these giants are watching over you, telling you what you can and cannot do.

Chances are this wouldn't instill a lot of confidence in you. In fact, you would probably feel a bit inferior. But let's back up even further. Take the newborn infant lying in the crib. He doesn't even know that he exists. He realizes something

"I paint what I see."

has happened. The lights are bright and something is different, but at this stage of development the infant literally does not know that he exists as a separate person. His central nervous system has not developed to the point where he can even tell the difference between himself and his mother.

Gradually this situation changes. The infant begins to recognize certain objects. He finds that some of these go with him everywhere he goes—for example, his hands, feet, and toes. He finds that others are not always present—chairs, blankets, and toys. He also finds that certain things (hands, feet, and toes) have a special kind of feeling. They are different from "other things." Slowly the infant begins to put this all together. He realizes that the feet, hands, and toes all belong to him. Finally, he comes to realize that he is a separate person—different from his mother and the world about him.

About this time, the average child takes his first few steps and utters his first real words. Soon after *dada* and *mama*, his favorite words become *me*, *my*, and *mine!* Now that he knows he is a separate person, he begins to gather his possessions to prove just who he is and what is his. By the time the child turns two, he is really getting to like the idea of being an independent person. When you say no, he says yes. When you say yes, he says no. When you say black, he says white. And when you say white, he says black. Whatever you say, your two-year-old is likely to take the opposite approach. This is why some call this period "the Terrible Twos." Two years ago this young person didn't even exist. One year ago he was just learning to move on his own and communicate with his first few words. Now, since he is a weak toddler living in a world of giants, one of the few ways he knows to demonstrate his strength is to do the opposite of what others say.

At about this time many parents decide to toilet train their youngsters. This can be a big mistake. We tell our child, "Mommy [or Daddy] wants you to do it in here when we tell you." The child thinks to himself, *I will do it in my pants anytime I please!* There are, he discovers, some things that even an eighteen-foot giant can't force him to do, and this is one of them. So we set the child on the potty and he just sits there. We let him stay for lengthy periods and nothing happens. Finally we give up, assuming that he doesn't really need to go. And five minutes later, what happens? Yes, he goes in his pants again!

Now what is the problem here? Does your child have a physical problem? Perhaps. Is he not bright enough to understand? I doubt it. Is he not physically ready to be trained? Maybe. But the chances are your child is simply taking this opportunity to prove that he has a mind of his own and doesn't always have to do what others tell him. He is trying to develop a sense of confidence—the second major emotional need.

Children with confidence feel good about their abilities. They can meet new people, speak up, express their desires, and freely interact with others. Children who lack confidence

Figure 3

God-Given Need:	When Need Is Not Met:	Child Turns to Substitute of:
Confidence	Weakness, Anxiety, Inferiority	Power

tend to feel tense, anxious, or inferior. Some withdraw and develop a quiet, unassuming, or dependent life-style. Others attempt to make up for their underlying lack of confidence by controlling others or becoming especially stubborn or self-willed.

Just like unmet needs for love, our children's needs for confidence can set another vicious cycle in motion. First they experience a God-given need for confidence. Next, we fail to recognize and help them meet that need. Finally, feeling inferior and lacking confidence, they turn to stubborn, belligerent, or controlling behaviors to gain a temporary feeling of strength and power.

Step by Step

Think of the dramatic changes infants must experience to change from tiny, helpless babies with absolutely no ability to exist without their mothers, into confident, mature, and independent individuals. First they have to learn that they exist. Then they have to learn to walk and talk. They have to learn to dress themselves, read and write, and get along with kids at school. They have to learn to protect themselves and satisfy the many adults who people their world. They face one task after another which must be mastered if they are going to feel good about themselves and their abilities. Each new task is a potential opportunity to feel inferior or inadequate.

Imagine how you might feel if you were suddenly placed in a strange world populated by eighteen-foot giants. You wouldn't know the language, you couldn't walk, and for several months you couldn't even feed yourself. How would you feel when you tried to take your first few faltering steps and fell? How would you feel when you tried to tie your shoelaces and couldn't quite do it? How would you feel when you went shopping or walking with your giant and he went so fast your little legs couldn't keep up, but he kept telling you, "Hurry up," "Keep up," or, "Don't dawdle"?

How might you feel when you went to school and had to learn to read and write and understand mathematics? What if some of your friends learned more easily than you and you felt embarrassed when you missed a problem or didn't understand? Or what if you weren't especially coordinated or good-looking? Meanwhile your eighteen-foot giants could do anything they wished. They also kept telling you what to do and anytime they didn't like what you were doing they could yell, "Stop that," "What's the matter?" or, "Can't you do anything right?"

When you turned twelve or thirteen you would feel even more awkward. You would start growing more quickly but your coordination and skills might lag beyond your body or—worse yet—those of your peers. Every time you tried something new you would compare yourself with your friends and each comparison would give you one more opportunity to feel inferior. On top of that, your giants would still be in the picture. Although you would be approaching them in size, they still would seem like giants to you. You might have to learn to drive a car with one of them peering over your shoulder warning you to "be careful," "watch out," "slow down," or "look both ways." Another one might be telling you how to act or look or what to do around the house.

Do you get the picture? For children, life is a series of challenges to meet in order to live confidently in a world of giants. I started feeling tired as I wrote this very partial list of tasks a child must master. Imagine how tiring it must be to actually learn them. In order to grow up feeling good about themselves, your sons and daughters must learn literally thousands of unfamiliar skills. They will need a lot of help if they are going to do this successfully and become confident, competent young men and women.

Confidence Killers

No parents want their children to suffer through a lifetime of feelings of inferiority, but if we aren't careful, we can unknowingly undermine our children's confidence as sure as if we tried. Take *criticism* for example. Most parents criticize their children at least occasionally. Some parents make a habit of it. Ernie was that way. A born perfectionist, Ernie wanted to be sure his daughter, Diane, did her best at school. When she was seven, I had the opportunity to observe Diane in her home. She was a very bright, alert young girl, but rather tense and quiet. At school she seemed withdrawn and depressed. I had recently given her an intelligence test in which she scored at the very top. Her IQ was over 160!

But when I observed her at home, I saw Diane's father trying to "help" her with her homework. "Here," he told Diane, "see where you went over the line? You can do better than that." Time after time Ernie pointed out his daughter's little failures and not once did he tell her how outstanding she was. My one-hour observation shed a lot of light on Diane's feelings of inferiority and depression at school.

Like some parents, Ernie assumed the best way to help his daughter was to criticize and correct her. But think how Diane must have felt. Here she was, a brilliant, well-behaved child who was working several years beyond her grade level and her father couldn't even affirm her and let her know how well she was doing. Although I haven't seen her since, I fear the constant drumbeat of her father's criticism left her with some lasting emotional damage.

Criticism is probably the single biggest obstacle to developing self-confidence. Criticism undercuts your sons' and daughters' confidence in themselves and makes them feel inadequate or inferior. I often tell parents it takes ninety-nine compliments to make up for one criticism. Whatever the ratio, I do know that most of us remember criticisms and "suggestions" long after we remember the positive things that others say about us. A psychologist friend of mine has a great antidote for parents who criticize their children. He teaches them this motto: "Catch them being good." In a very simple way this communicates a vital truth. Children gain more confidence when they receive positive attention for their successes than when they receive negative attention for their failures.

Comparing children with their siblings or other children also undermines their developing self-confidence. Children need to be valued for their special characteristics and affirmed for their success, not compared with others. Comparisons say, "You shouldn't be yourself and develop your unique abilities. You should be like someone else." Over a period of time this either creates resentment toward the child they are being compared with, feelings of inferiority, or both.

Worry and *overprotection* are other attitudes that can interfere with the development of your children's self-confidence. I know you want to protect your children from painful experiences and potential dangers. But parents who worry excessively or overprotect their children communicate this kind of message: "I lack confidence in you." "Be careful." "I don't think you can handle it." Each of these messages plants feelings of self-doubt in a young child's mind.

CONFIDENCE KILLERS

Worry can be a special problem when your children reach the teenage years. By then, they are starting to tackle some potentially dangerous activities like driving, working, and dating. Although we would like to trust our teenagers, most of us parents worry at least a little. If we couple memories of our own adolescent risk taking or irresponsibility with our children's past lapses and the horror stories we hear of adolescents, it's no wonder we worry. But remember, too many "reminders" say, "Honey, I don't trust you to be able to make good decisions." Your teenagers need some limits and guidance but they also need as much confidence as you can offer.[1]

Building Your Child's Self-Confidence

Developing self-confidence is a lengthy process that begins soon after birth. Once children have attached securely to their mothers and experienced her loving care, they are ready to start separating from her and testing out their own abilities. Your attitudes will probably be the main ingredient in your children's developing sense of confidence or lack of it.

Do you realize how fragile your children's feelings of confidence will be? Do you realize how sensitive they are to failure? Do you see your children's attitudes toward themselves as precious possessions? Are you committed to helping them feel good about themselves? For their sake and yours, make a commitment to help your sons and daughters see what beautiful, gifted children they are. I know it's easy to lose sight of this when they are fighting or causing you one hassle after another. But never forget that your children are created and gifted by God and always try to sensitively help them develop their abilities.

Encouragement is another key to increasing your child's self-confidence. Children need encouragement to venture out and

[1] Dr. Narramore has written two books for parents of teenagers. *Adolescence Is Not an Illness*, published by Fleming H. Revell, and *Cutting the Cord*, coauthored by Dr. Vern Lewis and published by Tyndale House.

try new things. If your daughter is afraid of failing, you may need to help her a bit at first. Work with her to slowly show how something is done. Help her get started. Then, as soon as she begins to understand, you can step aside and let her try it for herself. Try to avoid either of two extremes. Don't tell your children, "Go and do it," without offering encouragement and making sure they know how to proceed. And don't step in and do it for them. The first leaves children feeling overwhelmed and at a loss to know what to do. The second robs them of the opportunity to develop their own skills. Your children need a balance of help, encouragement, and the opportunity to do things for themselves.

Jan did this for her daughters. From the time they were preschoolers she taught them how to help around the house. They helped her dust and clean the house. They helped her pick flowers and arrange them. They helped in little ways in the kitchen. When her girls were teenagers, Jan took a job outside the home. By then, her girls could pretty well run things by themselves. They still needed Mom's encouragement, but they often fixed dinner for their mom and dad, cleaned the house, and even helped them entertain. Because they had worked along with their mom, they had plenty of confidence in their own abilities.

By contrast Esther did everything by herself around the house. She cooked and cleaned and told her friends it was easier to do things herself than teach her daughter. But years later, her daughter told me, "When I got married I hardly knew how to boil water. I still hate housework and everything I do feels like a tremendous struggle." If Esther had trained her daughter better she would have been a much happier and more competent adult.

Praise is a close relative of encouragement. It's a great way to catch your children being good. Take every opportunity to praise your sons' and daughters' efforts. Share in their excitement over their first "artwork." Tell them how great they're doing in their little jobs around the house. Thank them for their helpfulness and compliment them when they look especially nice or keep their room especially neat. Each compliment tells your children, "You have abilities. You are doing great. You can do it. You can succeed." This builds your children up and gives them courage to try even bigger challenges.

Some parents find it difficult to affirm their children. They feel uncomfortable or even a little dishonest saying, "That's great," when their children's work doesn't meet their own standards. If you grew up in a home where there was little encouragement, you may be that way yourself. But remember, children gain motivation to do better when they are affirmed, not when they are criticized.

Don decided he was going to overcome his discomfort about complimenting his children by saying at least one positive thing to each of his children every day. At first he felt uncomfortable. But with encouragement from his wife and friends, Don kept at it. Sometimes he had to struggle to find anything that merited his perfectionistic approval. But in time he became much freer with his feelings of appreciation and eventually he felt totally comfortable telling his kids how great they were!

I'm not saying you should compliment your children insincerely or act as if they are better than someone else. Children sense it if we say, "That's great," to everything they do. But children need some affirmation even when the results of their efforts are less than perfect. We need to affirm their steps in the right direction instead of waiting until they have arrived.

And we need to affirm their efforts as well as their successes. You know how it feels when you have a huge task ahead of you. By yourself, it can be a long, difficult chore, but if someone drops by to admire your work or encourage you, you gain a second wind and strength to keep on going. If we adults need praise and affirmation, think how much more our children must.

Unfortunately, not all praise is helpful. A couple of years ago I was bodysurfing at the beach and I noticed a man with his son—a boy about nine years of age. Every time the boy caught a wave, his father complimented him. He would say, "That's good!" or "That's great!" At first I was impressed. I thought, *It's great that that father is complimenting his son on his surfing.* Then I noticed something interesting: Every time the boy came out of the water after catching a wave, he turned to his dad and asked, "How did I do, Dad?" or, "How was that?" In other words, his first thought was on the quality of his performance. Not once did he come out of the water and say, "That was a great one!" or, "Boy, I sure enjoyed that one!"

In complimenting his son, this father had subtly shifted the focus of his bodysurfing from enjoyment to performance. Surfing became another opportunity for the boy to please his father or perform well instead of simply a chance to enjoy himself. That dad was giving his son a great gift of meaningful time together, and I don't want to minimize that gift. But in a way I am sure he didn't understand, he might have also been subtly undermining some of his son's feelings of enjoyment by focusing his praise excessively on his boy's performance.

I don't share this little incident to discourage you from praising your children. I am simply suggesting that there are different ways of encouraging your sons and daughters. Try to keep in mind their need for a sense of *inner* satisfaction and enjoyment as well as their need to master new skills. When your children are enjoying themselves and happy with their achievements, try to share their joy and fulfillment rather than calling attention to the performance aspects of their activities. Intersperse comments like "Hey, that looks like great fun!" or "You must have really enjoyed that one!" between occasional comments like "You're doing great!" Comments like this show your children that you like to see them enjoying life and help offset the attitude prevalent in our society that performance is more important than inner feelings of satisfaction and contentment.

Danger: Power Struggle Ahead

Several years ago I called our son in from play to go to his grandmother's house for dinner. "I'm *not* going!" Dickie emphatically announced. My first impulse was to say, "Oh, yes, you are! You come in here right now!" He had challenged my authority, and I was prepared to show him who was boss. I quickly caught myself, however, and realized what was going on. Dickie was enjoying himself and didn't want to be disturbed. The last thing on his mind was going to Grandmother's for supper. I also realized that he was about to draw me into a fight. He had issued a challenge, and I was ready to do battle. But knowing these conflicts never have a happy ending, I backed off.

With strong feeling, I said, "You really don't want to go to Grandmother's, do you?"

"No!" he said firmly, but with less anger. "I'm not going!"

"Are we interrupting your game?" I inquired.

"Yes," he said, "and I want to finish."

"I understand that, Dickie," I replied. "Sometimes I have to do something I don't want, and I get angry too. I know it's hard to stop your game, and Mom and Dad should have reminded you earlier. But we told Grandmother we would be over at six. We have to leave now." Still unhappy, but a bit more understanding, Dickie said, "Oh, all right," and came into the house and prepared to leave.

Dickie had just about sucked me into a power struggle. A power struggle is essentially a fight for control between a parent and a child.[2] We ask a child to do something and he refuses; we ask him to stop doing something and he continues. In one way or another he is bound and determined to "show us who is boss."

These power struggles have two causes. One is your child's need for confidence. Because children are weak and small in relation to us, they naturally want to find ways of improving their confidence and showing that they have some control over their own lives. This is a natural and God-given desire. Nobody likes to feel like a helpless puppet in someone else's show.

Along with this healthy desire is a less noble one. Since the time of Adam and Eve, all human beings have had a tendency to want things their own way. We don't just want to have a healthy sense of confidence. We prefer to do everything *we* want. If we had our way, we wouldn't have anybody telling us anything to do. In other words, we would like the complete power to control our own lives.

[2] Rudolf Dreikurs and Vicki Soltz popularized the concept of the power struggle in their helpful book *Children: The Challenge* (New York: Hawthorn, 1964). Unfortunately they hold a humanistic view of human nature that sees children as essentially good (or at least neutral) and consequently propound a democratic form of family government rather than a loving, sensitive authority.

This combination of our children's need for confidence and their desire to be their own boss can trigger all sorts of conflicts. Time after time, your children's first response to your directions may be to do the opposite or resist. If you want to avoid a thousand hassles like this, you must learn to recognize when your sons and daughters are drawing you into a power struggle and remove yourself before the battle begins. Your goal should not be to win a fight or prove that you are the boss. Your goal should simply be to get your children to obey while preserving their self-respect and good feelings about themselves.

With a little practice you can do this for your children. Begin by becoming sensitive to your own feelings of frustration. The moment you start becoming angry with your child, watch out. The chances are you will soon want to show him who is boss, and once that happens you are headed for a fight no one will win. When Dickie told me he wasn't going to his grandmother's, my first tendency was to fight fire with fire. At that point I could have easily forced Dickie to "get in here," to show him I was boss. But think how he would have felt. He would have felt angry, misunderstood, and disrespected. How would you like it if an eighteen-foot giant came up to you in the middle of your game or television program and announced, "You have to stop now. We are going"? Nobody likes to be interrupted in the middle of an interesting activity, and nobody likes to be bossed around by an insensitive giant.

Once you restrain your first impulse to join the battle, you are on your way. Next, find out how your children are feeling and why they need to be so stubborn. When I realized Dickie was in the middle of a game, I could sympathize with his reaction. We hadn't prepared him by reminding him a half hour before we had to leave that he would have to finish up his game.

Some children react stubbornly because we give our orders like a colonel. Instead of quietly reminding them it's time to go, we sternly tell them to stop what they are doing and come with us. Other children develop an especially negative pattern because their parents give too many orders or nag or remind them too much. Children need limits and direction, but they don't need omnipresent giants controlling every area of their lives.

Once you let your children know you understand and respect their feelings, you can usually go ahead and see that they carry through on your instructions. But you can do that calmly instead of challenging them in anger. Simply tell them, "I know you don't like it, honey, but today we have to do this." By handling your children's challenges this way you can preserve their sense of confidence while still getting them to cooperate. Instead of winning over them with your power, you can win them over by your sensitivity and understanding.

Chapter Highlights

Confidence is the second major God-given emotional need. Children who lack confidence feel tense, anxious, inferior, or inadequate. In order to ward off these unpleasant emotions, many children become stubborn, bossy, or controlling.

You can help your children develop confidence by avoiding criticism, overprotection, and comparisons with their siblings. Instead, value their abilities and give them plenty of affirmation and encouragement. Praise, appropriate responsibilities, and opportunities to have "success experiences" are the keys to developing appropriate self-confidence.

5
Is Your Child "Too Good"?

You probably know at least one perfectionistic housewife. If you arrive thirty minutes early for a formal dinner she is there waiting for you with everything in its place. The table is set, the food is in the oven, and the kids are dressed and taken care of. At a time when most of us would be running around in a dither, she has everything under control. Even when you just "drop by," her house is in order. And she manages all of that with three young children, along with serving on a couple of committees at church or school.

You also may know a few workaholics. They are the first to arrive at work and the last to leave. They bring work home in the evenings and on weekends. When vacations roll around, they wonder whether they can afford to get away. If they finally do manage to take a few days off, they very carefully plan their entire vacation. They want to be sure they keep busy and they don't want to "waste time." Just camping out or relaxing is hard for them. They become nervous if they aren't busy, so they get up and check the tent stakes, drive to the nearest town and fill the car with gas, or call back to the office "just to check on things." After a few days they are anxious to return home and get back to work.

This performance-oriented, workaholic style of life is so common in our society that we frequently fail to recognize what lies behind it. Actually, most workaholics and perfectionists are suffering from the lack of a third hidden emotional need. Deep down they lack a settled sense of significance and worth and value. They don't really feel good about themselves so they have to work incessantly to prove their value and satisfy their craving for significance. At the end of every day they think, *Today I did this, this, and this. Therefore I must be okay.*

When people like this suffer a heart attack or in some other way are physically incapacitated, they invariably go into a serious depression. Since their feelings of personal worth and value are so wrapped up in their performance, they suddenly lose their foundation for good feelings about themselves. They can no longer look at their day's performance and say, "Look at all I've done. I must be a valuable person." Consequently their hidden feelings of insignificance, worthlessness, or guilt rise up to the surface.

The God-given need for a sense of worth or value is the third cornerstone of your child's adjustment. Children whose needs for a sense of worth are met feel good about themselves and others. They believe they are valuable or significant people. They head into life with hope and optimism. And they believe their thoughts and feelings and opinions count.

Children who lack a solid conviction of their worth or value are prone to depression and guilt. They can feel incredibly bad whenever they fall short of your expectations or their own or God's. Instead of experiencing normal feelings of regret and a healthy desire to do better, they mentally flagellate themselves for their failures or repeatedly tell themselves how terrible and awful they are. In Christian families, these children often have serious struggles in their relationships with God. They want to please Him, but they feel like such failures they are convinced that God can't forgive them. As teenagers they may make repeated commitments or rededications and vow to do better, but before long they cave in to their feelings of guilt once more.

Some Christian parents have a difficult time helping these children develop a sense of worth. They know the Bible teaches that we are sinful, and they don't want to obscure their children's sinfulness by stressing their worth or value. In fact, some Christian parents feel uncomfortable or even guilty affirming their children and telling them how great they are. They are afraid their children will become proud or forget that they are sinners. But feelings of worth are very different from pride or denying one's sins. We are all significant to God and valuable in His eyes even though we are sinful. He created us in His image. He sent His Son, Christ, to die for us. And we will spend eternity with Him. We aren't righteous, and we need to be aware of our sinfulness, but we are of great value and significance to God.

Feelings of worth are related to feelings of confidence but they are a little different. Confidence relates to our performance and our ability to function competently. Feelings of worth relate more to our basic sense of value as a person. Although both a lack of confidence and a lack of worth may motivate us to excessive striving, their purposes are different. When children lack confidence they become competitive, power-oriented, or passive in order to control others and gain a sense of strength or avoid failing. When they lack feelings of self-worth, they attempt to achieve in order to demonstrate that they really are valuable, significant, or worthwhile.

The Perfectionistic Child

The lack of a God-given sense of worth and value sets our now familiar cycle in motion. First, children experience the need to feel like valuable, significant individuals. Next, a series of events or problems in relating to important people undermines their sense of worth. Finally, if they don't simply cave in to those bad feelings, they turn to overachievement or pressure-driven goodness to try to wipe away the distressing feelings of badness. Figure 4 shows that sequence.

Figure 4

God-Given Need:	When Need Is Not Met:	Child Turns to Substitute of:
Worth	Unworthiness, Bad Behavior, Unimportance	Performance, Perfection

Perfectionistic children are among the clearest examples of people trying to compensate for the lack of a deep inner sense of worth. Striving to please their parents, others in authority, or their own demanding expectations, they are often among the top students in their class. They study diligently and are polite, cooperative, and likable. In fact, many parents would give anything if they had such well-behaved children. But beneath their cooperative and achieving front lies a different story. These children are continually working to prove their adequacy and worth. They are under incredible inner pressure, and their performance grows more out of their bad feelings about themselves than from a healthy desire to develop their God-given gifts. By meeting every conceivable expectation of their parents and others, they hope to earn a sense of value as a person.

Unfortunately, this driven perfectionism robs them of much of the freedom and happiness that should accompany the childhood years. Instead of feeling free to relax and play and enjoy themselves, they always have to work or study. When these children reach adolescence, they typically move in one of two directions. Some continue their self-inflicted pressure and become involved in one school activity after another. They study for hours at a time, join every club imaginable, and if they attend church, are equally involved there. Sometimes they put themselves under such intense pressure that they finally cave in, have a "nervous breakdown," or even turn to suicide to escape their feelings of guilt and worthlessness.

Other pressured adolescents take precisely the opposite tack. Having spent years trying to be good, they are finally fed up. They have followed their parents' advice. They have followed their teachers' advice. And if they are Christians, they have sincerely attempted to follow the will of God. They have confessed their sins, read their Bible regularly, and tried to be good Christians. But their lack of an inner sense of worth makes it very difficult for them to believe God is ever pleased with them. They temporarily feel better after confessing their sins, but their feelings of worthlessness soon rise up to erase their short-lived experiences of forgiveness.

After repeated attempts at gaining inner peace by pleasing God and others, these adolescents eventually give up. They decide it is futile to continue seeking a sense of self-worth through being good, so they start rebelling against their parents, their teachers, their church leaders, and even God. They decide their parents' standards are unrealistic, their morality and ethics are useless, and Christianity isn't all it's cracked up to be. Consequently, they throw off all their standards and decide to live it up. Since perfectionism and performance didn't get them what they needed, they try the opposite.

Mirror, Mirror, on the Wall

No parent wakes up in the morning thinking, *What can I do to undermine my children's feelings of worth and value,* but sometimes we unknowingly do that very thing. I once read an article that showed how that can happen. It went something like this:

> What if we talked to our friends the way we talk to our children? Our friends, Fred and Millie, would arrive for dinner and our conversation would go like this.
>
> "It's about time you got here, Fred. You're late again. Well, come on in and close the door. Were you born in a barn?

"Sit down over here on the couch. Now remember, don't put your feet on the coffee table. You know what a fool you made of yourself the last time.

"Okay, let's eat. Everybody have a seat. Now you have to have a little bit of everything even if you don't like it. Be careful with your drink, Fred. You know how clumsy you are. No, you can't have dessert until you've cleaned up everything on your plate. And you're going to sit there until you are finished."

Needless to say, we would never speak to our friends this way! It is obviously disrespectful. But isn't this exactly the way many of us speak to our children day in and day out? I know we don't intend to undermine our children's positive feelings about themselves, but think about it. Do your daily interactions build up and affirm your children or do they tend to accuse them and put them down? To your children, you are the first mirror that reflects a picture of who they are and what they are worth. Every time your sons and daughters look into your face or listen to your tone of voice they see a picture of themselves through you. When they hear endearing, pleasing words, they know you value them and like them. This builds a picture of themselves as lovable, valuable, and worthwhile people.

But when you lash out at your children or tell them, "You're clumsy," "You are always late," or, "You don't have sense enough to eat a decent meal," you project an entirely different picture. You make them look bad, evil, or unintelligent. Children who hear many messages like this start wondering if there isn't something fundamentally wrong or bad about them. In the rest of this chapter we will look at several things you can do to give your children a clear picture of their worth and avoid undermining their fragile sense of self-esteem.

Building Your Child's Self-Esteem

When my wife and I were younger, we were a one-car family. Kathy and the children picked me up from work in the afternoon; I would climb into the front seat next to Kathy while the children moved to the back. I would say hi to the kids, give them a hug, and promptly begin a conversation with my wife. We'd talk about Kathy's activities and mine, but rarely did we speak directly to Dickie and Debbie. They were supposed to sit quietly in the back for fifteen minutes as we discussed "important" matters.

Typically Dickie and Debbie would sit quietly for a few minutes and then begin to fuss or fight. By the time we were halfway home they would really be upset. Finally we realized what was happening. By leaving the children out of our conversation, we were essentially telling them they were unimportant. Their thoughts and wishes and reports about their days would have to wait until Mom and Dad were finished. The trouble was, Mom and Dad usually didn't finish until we were safely home and ready for dinner. And even then we often continued to monopolize the conversation.

When we saw what we were doing, we started bringing Dickie and Debbie into our conversations. We decided that as adults, our talk could usually wait. So we asked the kids about their day. When we did discuss my work or Kathy's activities, we tried to do it in ways that the children could understand. Before long Dickie and Debbie were feeling like a much more integral part of our family and of much more significance to their parents. Besides that, they fought less while riding in the car. *The first way to give your children a sense of worth or value is to involve them in your family conversations and value their interests and activities.*

Gee, Mom, She Thinks I'm Real!

Some time ago I heard a story of a family that went out to dinner at a restaurant. The waitress asked the young boy of the family, "What would you like to eat, sonny?" "I'll have a hamburger," the boy proudly replied. But his mother looked sternly at the waitress and announced, "He will have the roast beef." Again directing her attention to the child, the waitress asked, "And what would you like on your hamburger?" "I'll have mustard and ketchup," the boy replied with a look of surprise. But again the mother interrupted to say, "He will have some green beans."

Ignoring the mother once more, the waitress continued, "And what would you like to drink?" "I'll have a Coke!" the little boy answered confidently. The mother sternly stated, "He will have some milk!"

The waitress left and in a few minutes returned with exactly what the little boy had ordered. He looked at his mother in amazement and said, "Gee, Mom, she thinks I'm real!"

This apocryphal story communicates another way of building your children's sense of worth and self-esteem. *Children feel better about themselves when we take their opinions seriously and let them make their own decisions.* Too many parents treat their children like second-class citizens. They say, "You're just a child, you wouldn't understand," or, "Wait till you grow up."

They go through life acting as if their children are somehow different and less important than adults.

If you want your children to develop a full appreciation of their significance as human beings, value their opinions and ideas. Whether it is choosing the clothes they will wear, the food they will eat, the color of your new car, the best professional football player, the church you will attend, or some political issue, your children need a chance to voice their opinions and know that you will take them seriously. Nothing tells a person he or she is more important than having someone listen to his or her ideas and value them as important.

Even though your children may not have the maturity to make the best decisions, you need to solicit their opinions and bring them into your decision making as much as possible. That's the way they learn. It also helps lay the foundation for a lasting sense of self-worth and self-esteem.

Gloria and Daniel did this for their children. It was time to purchase a new car and Daniel wanted an economy car since he had to pay the gas bills. Gloria thought they needed a station wagon since she had to transport the entire family, the groceries, and the several other odds and ends that find their way into the family vehicle. Their girls, Bethany and Becky, just wanted a nice car with plenty of room in the backseat and a pleasing color.

Each time Gloria and Daniel looked at a new car, they asked Bethany and Becky to try out the backseat. The children told their mom and dad whether the legroom was adequate or too tight. They checked out the storage space behind the backseat because their equipment would have to fit there. And they gave their opinions about color and other issues.

At one point Gloria and Daniel agreed on a small station wagon. It had plenty of space, four doors, and got good mileage. But when the girls tried out the backseat they said in unison, "It's too crowded back here." Their parents' first reaction was to get in and try it for themselves. They were sure they could scrunch up in there and if they could, so could their children! But then they realized they would be ignoring their daughters' input. Bethany and Becky were the ones who would spend half of their growing lives back there, not their mom and dad. Since the night was young, Gloria and Daniel decided to look some more. If they couldn't find another car that met everyone's need, someone would have to sacrifice and they might go ahead with the station wagon. But if they could, they wanted to respond to their children's input.

Just down the street was another dealer, so they checked out his model. It was about the same price as the first car, and as soon as Bethany and Becky climbed in the back they said, "This is better." After checking everything else out, they bought the second car and everyone was happy. The car was slightly larger than Daniel had planned, slightly smaller than Gloria had originally hoped for, but it had plenty of room for two children and a host of their things in the backseat. Everyone came away feeling they had made a good decision and they had made it as a family. Daniel told me later that he wasn't sure there was any more space in the backseat of the second car than in the first but the important thing for him was how his children felt.

Gloria and Daniel helped their girls meet three of their God-given needs that night. The girls felt loved as they spent time with their mom and dad. They gained confidence as they saw how their parents shopped for cars and participated in the process. And they felt valuable and significant since their opinions were respected.

I am not suggesting that you abdicate your parental responsibility and turn all of the decision making over to your children. If Gloria and Daniel's girls thought they had to have a Cadillac, that would not have worked. But even then, I suspect that Gloria and Daniel would have listened carefully and respectfully to their girls' ideas and explained why they couldn't afford (or didn't want) to spend their money on such an expensive car. I am also not suggesting you operate your family on the basis of a democracy or the "one man, one vote rule" that some psychologists propose. You may leave some decisions entirely up to your children. You will certainly make some decisions yourself. And there may be times when everyone has a say. I am simply suggesting that you can demonstrate your respect for your children in tangible ways by valuing their thoughts, wishes, and feelings, and involving them in your family's planning.

Some parents are afraid this will spoil their children or make them always want to have their way. Actually the opposite is true. Children who are involved in their family's planning learn to share and cooperate. They also have an easier time making the transition from the dependency of childhood to the independency of adulthood. Since they have had experience shopping for cars or carpets or clothes and giving their input around the house, they have had good practice making decisions. Children whose parents don't respect their opinions or fail to bring them into their families' decisions in their younger years don't know how to share cooperatively later. Since they have never had a chance to make their own decisions, they feel they must fight to get their way or make their decisions by themselves the way their parents did.

A Language of Love

A third key to instilling a positive sense of self-worth in your children is to develop a language of love and deep respect. Avoid all name-calling, labeling, and character assignation. Words like *stupid, lazy,* or *worthless* can become fixed ingredients in a growing child's self-concept. Instead, develop an endearing vocabulary for your children. Tell them often, "I appreciate you," "That's a great idea," "You're neat," and, "We're so glad you are our son [or daughter]." Your tone of voice communicates as much as your words themselves. Angry, condemning, or derogatory tones chip away at your children's positive feelings about themselves. Kindly spoken and respectful words help your children develop solid feelings of self-worth.

The way you discipline your children also affects their developing self-esteem. Impulsive punishment and punishment done in anger frightens children and makes them feel bad or worthless. Even when this kind of punishment brings the behavior changes you desire, it undercuts your son's and daughter's sense of dignity and self-respect. They may end up behaving well but feeling miserable. Gentle and encouraging words coupled with firm but loving correction tell children, "You are good, but we have to work on your behavior." This lets children feel respected at the same time they are corrected.

Christian parents have an added resource for helping children feel good about themselves. The Bible says we are created in God's image, that we are gifted by God, that Christ died for us, and that we will spend eternity with Him. *As your children learn they are special to God they will find it easier to realize they can be special to others and that they are important, significant individuals.*

Chapter Highlights

All children are born with a God-given need to feel significant, valuable, and important. When that need isn't met,
children either become depressed or turn to driven performance to try to fight off their feelings of worthlessness. You
can help your children feel better about themselves by treat-
ing them with respect, bringing them into family discussions,
valuing their ideas, speaking to them in endearing, affirming
words, and telling them often how valuable and important
they are to you and to God.

6
"I'm Bored!"

One Saturday afternoon I was working at our dining room table when suddenly something outside the window caught my eye. Looking up, I saw our son marching back and forth with a two-by-three-foot picket sign. In big, bold letters he had written "I AM BORED!" When Dickie knew he had my attention, a huge smile spread across his face. I began to laugh, and so did he. After calling my wife over to view our "labor-management" problems, I dropped my work and went outside to talk with our "picket."

"Dad," Dickie said, "I'm bored." I gave him a big hug, told him how cute his sign was, and said, "Let's go inside and talk this over." After a little discussion, Dickie and I decided to go downtown for a soft drink and check out a new restaurant I was thinking of taking Kathy to. Usually Dickie and Debbie are not so cute when they are bored. In fact, they are more likely to start fighting when they are bored than at any other time.

Along with needs for love, confidence, and worth, all children also need interesting activities to challenge them and occupy their time. Constructive activities enrich children's lives and give them something to look forward to. They expand their horizons and let them practice new or familiar skills.

When children lack constructive activities they turn to destructive activities. Next to the search for attention, I suspect the search for destructive activities causes more problems in young children than any other thing. Your children's reactions on a rainy day are a good example. Chances are they will ask you a thousand times, "Mother, what can I do?" But no matter what you suggest, they soon become disinterested and bored. They feel cooped up, inhibited, and deprived of any constructive active outlets for their energy. And since they are bored, you can expect one interruption after another or some trouble with their siblings.

Figure 5 shows this cycle. First the child experiences a God-given need for interesting activities. Second, if that need is not met she feels bored. Finally, she turns to negative behavior to stir up some kind of stimulating, substitute activity to ward off her boredom.

One of Those Days

During a question time at an all-day-Saturday seminar for parents a young mother asked, "What should we do with a child who is constantly climbing the walls?" I decided to try out my psychological understanding of children so I answered her question with a question. "Is he two, and do you live in an apartment?" I asked. Almost jumping off her chair, the mother replied, "How did you know?"

Figure 5

God-Given Need:	When Need Is Not Met:	Child Turns to Substitute of:
Constructive Activity	Boredom	Destructive Activity

Actually my "insight" was very simple. Infants don't climb walls and older children and children with an entire house and yard to roam around in find it easier to occupy themselves. But two-year-olds who are cooped up in limited space do climb walls!

If you were a toddler in a world of giants wouldn't you want to go exploring? And if you had very limited space to explore, wouldn't you soon become bored and start climbing walls? Children like this are not maladjusted and they aren't misbehaving; they also don't need discipline or punishment. They are simply bored stiff in their limited environment and need a place to run and play. They also may need some friends to play with. Until these needs are met, they are going to act like "problem children" even though they aren't.

Boredom is one of the main reasons most families occasionally have their "bad days." In fact, don't you find that you can almost predict which days of the week will go better than others or certain times of the day when your children are more likely to get into trouble? Some children are fine on Saturdays, for example, because they have cartoons in the morning and their parents in the afternoon. Others are horrible on Saturday because there is nothing going on that interests them. Some families enjoy peaceful, relaxed times on Sundays. Others find Sundays are chaotic. Some children do well on Mondays and Tuesdays, but by midweek they are starting to get fussy and on your nerves. Others do fine for an hour or so after school but start getting upset by four or five in the afternoon. Every child seems to develop his or her own rhythm.

Plan Ahead

Early in our family life I assumed Dickie and Debbie should be responsible for finding ways to occupy their time. I thought, *Kathy and I are busy and the children ought to be able to think of things they would like to do.* But although my assumption made a lot of sense to me, I found that young children didn't work that way. Periodically they would say, "Daddy, I'm bored," or, "What can we do?" And if I didn't help them find an interesting activity, they would keep pestering me or begin to tease and fight each other.

Finally I talked the situation over with my wife. We discussed the way we felt when we were bored and what it took to get us out of periods of boredom. Usually it was people or an interesting activity. Reading a book, watching another television program, or being told to "find something to do" didn't help.

Once we realized this, we decided to try to stop whatever we were doing long enough to sit down with our children, allow them to express their feelings of boredom or dissatisfaction, and see what we could do to help. We could usually help them out of their boredom with just a few minutes of well-spent time and planning. We also found we could bypass most of these troubled times if we helped our children plan their days ahead of time. Kathy was great at this. She loves to plan so she can look forward to things. Each week she thought through the children's activities and our own. If Dickie and Debbie had plenty of activities and if she and I had some time together, she let it go at that. But if she sensed the children might not have much time with their friends in the ordinary course of the week, she encouraged them to invite a friend over some afternoon or evening, or suggested we plan a night out or set up a family evening. In this way we all had something to look forward to. Special times actually have a two-fold value. Your children love them and enjoy them, and they also spend hours or days ahead of time happily anticipating the activities. Their anticipation eradicates a lot of boredom!

We also learned to plan ahead for weekends. Sometimes there was plenty going on. School functions, soccer games, invitations to friends' homes, swimming, or just neighborhood playtimes kept everyone occupied. But if we sensed things were going to go slow we talked it over with Dickie and Debbie and discussed something they could do or something we could do together. The activity was inconsequential; the important thing was that we found something everyone enjoyed.

When your children have their bored, frustrated times, you had better have some plans in mind unless you want continuous trouble. In fact, it's best to plan your days so that these times *never* arrive. If your children usually become bored and upset at a predictable time of the day or week, sit down and find out why. Are they tired of playing with their siblings? Are they tired of being left out of your "adult" activities? Are they tired of the routine of school? Once you know the "hidden" reasons for their feelings of frustration, you can help them plan some interesting activities.

Teenagers react to boredom in slightly different ways than younger children. Sometimes they mope around the house making everyone else share their misery. Other times they seek out their friends and begin looking for stimulating activities. Unfortunately, "stimulating" may mean taking a chance, pushing the limits of good judgment, reckless driving, pranks, or experimenting with alcohol or drugs. All of these activities are fair game for bored teenagers looking for exciting substitutes for constructive activities.

Because of the strong tendency for teenagers to seek out dangerous experiences, it is important to do everything in your power to see that your teenagers have a variety of healthy, challenging activities and friends. An active church youth group is one of the best ways to combat this potential problem. Inviting their friends over and supporting their extracurricular activities are other ways of engaging them in constructive activities and avoiding boredom and the dangerous substitute activities that can result from it.

What About My Needs?

In the past four chapters I have talked about the urgency of spending time with your children, helping them plan their days, and seeing that they have plenty of constructive activities to keep them busy. By now you may be asking, "But what about my needs? I need a little time to myself. I can't drop everything I am doing and run to my children's sides every time they utter a peep."

That's true. And in fact, you shouldn't. You are not your children's servant, and you don't have to always be at their beck and call. You shouldn't let them constantly interrupt your activities and you shouldn't train them to think that they should never have to wait. If you don't set some limits and let your children know that you need some time for yourself, you will be doing both your children and yourself a big disservice. Your children won't learn that other people have needs too, and you will become so frustrated you won't be able to give to your children when you do have time.

All I am saying is this: The time you spend playing and sharing with your children and helping them plan some interesting activities will save you time in the long run. Thirty minutes of planning or fun together can save hours of interruptions, hassles, and crying later. Instead of waiting for a problem to happen, why not sidestep it with a little planning or prevention? If you add up the amount of time you spend correcting your children, stopping fights, and handling interruptions, it will probably amount to a good bit more time than it would take to have some quality moments together ahead of time.

Let's say you are on the phone, talking with a friend in your living room, or in the middle of your work. At precisely the wrong moment your daughter comes up to you and asks a question or tells you she is bored. She obviously has a need or problem. She is feeling bored, left out (and consequently unloved or unimportant), or both. But you also have some needs. You need to complete your work or you need some uninterrupted time with your friend. What can you do that will satisfy your needs as well as your daughter's?

Usually you can solve both problems with a simple four-step plan. First, if at all possible, stop what you are doing for just a moment or two to see what the problem is. Look your daughter directly in the eyes and let her know that for that moment she has your full attention. Second, hear her out. Ask her if she is feeling left out or bored and let her express her feelings. Third, help her find something that stimulates her interest. Sometimes inviting another child to your home will occupy her time. Since you have a friend visiting, why can't she? Sometimes television will serve as a short-term electronic baby-sitter. Or sometimes a newspaper to cut up will help!

Finally, if you are convinced she has plenty of appealing things to do or if you just cannot be interrupted at the moment, tell her when you can help her and why you cannot just now. You might say, "I know you are feeling bored, honey, and I would like to help. But right now I am stirring this recipe, and it will burn if I don't finish it." Or tell her, "Mother is talking to Janice right now. We will be through when the big hand of the clock gets up to here. Then you and I can have some time together. I know you want to do something right now but if you keep playing school [or dolls or watching TV] for a few more minutes, Mommy will be with you."

Sometimes even this won't do it. As one mother put it, "My son continually wants attention. I read him a story, give him love, and then explain that I am busy. But he continues to want attention and nag me. It seems like children are basically selfish and want more attention than anyone can give!"

Young children do have short attention spans and some children do want more attention than any parent can give. When this happens, once you have done all you can, ignore

their interruptions or, if they become destructive or obnox-
ious, lovingly but firmly send or take them to their rooms.
Take them seriously and let them know that you want to help
when you have time but they must still respect your needs.
When your children learn you will keep your word and aren't
just putting them off, they will usually find some way to get
by until you are free. If not, a little time alone in their room
may help.

Chapter Highlights

Your sons and daughters need plenty of interesting, challenging activities to liven up their days. If they lack these
constructive activities they will become restless and bored. In
turn, they will get into trouble in order to replace their boredom with a little excitement. You can enrich your children's
lives and help them avoid a lot of destructive misbehaviors by
seeing to it that they have plenty of enjoyable, constructive
activities to occupy their time.

Part III
Why Children Misbehave

7
When Hidden Needs Aren't Met

Tom and Marsha stopped me after a PTA meeting to discuss a problem they had with their son. They hadn't been married long, and it was the second marriage for Marsha. Although it had been more than two years since her first marriage ended, Mark, her oldest child, was not getting along with his stepfather at all. Even though Tom was sensitive to the children and wasn't forcing himself on them, Mark reacted negatively. He refused to go places with his stepfather. He refused to say more than a few words. And in general, he was nasty and resentful.

As we talked, it was apparent that Mark saw his stepfather as an intruder and was blaming him for his parents' breakup. Mark's rejection of his stepfather was a way of expressing his anger and gaining revenge for the hurt he had suffered from his parents' divorce.

Genesis tells another story of a family conflict:

> Joseph, a young man of seventeen, was tending the
> flocks with his brothers, . . . and he brought their father
> a bad report about them. Now Israel loved Joseph more
> than any of his other sons, because he had been born to
> him in his old age; and he made a richly ornamented
> robe for him. When his brothers saw that their father
> loved him more than any of them, they hated him and
> could not speak a kind word to him.
>
> Genesis 37:2–4

Joseph's tattling on his brothers, a couple of his dreams,
and his father's favoritism, combined to stir up his brothers'
resentment. They were so angry they decided they would
murder Joseph, toss him into a well, and tell their father a
wild animal had attacked and eaten him. Fortunately, Joseph's oldest brother, Reuben, offered an alternative. He
suggested they simply throw Joseph into the well alive, ap-
parently with the idea of returning to rescue him later. About
this time, the brothers noticed a caravan coming on its way to
Egypt and decided to sell Joseph as a slave. That way they
wouldn't suffer the guilt of murder and would have twenty
pieces of silver for their efforts.

The Search for Revenge

Mark's rejection of his stepfather and the scheming of Joseph's brothers were both motivated by a desire for revenge.
This is a fifth common cause of children's misbehavior. When
your children's needs for love, confidence, worth, and constructive activity go unmet, your children don't only reach for
the substitutes of attention, power and control, perfectionism
and performance, and destructive activity. They also become

resentful and seek ways to get even with whoever has failed to meet their emotional needs. Along with misbehaving to gain attention, for example, children who feel unloved usually become angry at the one from whom they desire love. Teenage girls who become pregnant out of wedlock, for example, are sometimes seeking the attention of men because they don't feel loved and close to their fathers. But getting pregnant can also serve another purpose. What upsets parents more than finding out their daughter is going to be an unwed mother? At an unconscious level, some love-starved girls get pregnant partly to express their anger at their parents. Getting pregnant is a way of punishing their parents for not loving them properly.

In a similar way, children lacking confidence may get into repeated power struggles, not only to try to prove their strength or gain power over their parents, but also to make life miserable for their mom and dad. Fighting and resisting become ways of expressing anger to the parents they believe have criticized or chopped them down and undermined their confidence. They try to get even with their eighteen-foot-giant parents by making them feel like helpless failures.

In much the same way, children lacking a sense of worth often turn to perfectionistic behavior. But they may also give up entirely. By quitting, they gain revenge on their parents for failing to make them feel a positive sense of worth. They may unconsciously reason, for example, *Since Mom and Dad already think I'm no good, I may as well live up* [or more accurately, *down*] *to their expectations. That will show them.*

The desire to gain revenge is at the root of many of your children's feelings of anger and frustration. In fact, revenge is one of the primary motivating forces behind anger. When someone hurts us, either physically or emotionally, we want to even the score and see them suffer a little in return! This is one reason children slam the door when they are sent to their room for discipline, or stick out their tongue, or sass us. They know that their negative reactions will upset us, and that is precisely what they intend!

Figure 6

God-Given Needs	When Needs Go Unmet	Child Turns to Revenge

Many adults do the same thing. If someone criticizes us or makes a hostile put-down, we return the favor. Or if our mates ignore us, we ignore them to let them know how it feels. The search for revenge wears a thousand disguises. Some children do poorly at school to irritate their parents. The more important grades are to their parents, the more the children know they can upset them by doing poorly. If a C will panic their parents, think what a D might do!

Other children become passively resistant to get even. If an eighteen-foot giant is always telling you to hurry up, think how you might upset her by slowing down! Some adolescents run away from home to say, "You don't meet my needs, so I'll show you what a lousy parent you are!" At the same time they temporarily escape their pain, they also get revenge on their parents. Teenagers whose parents are committed Christians may rebel against their Christian training in order to express deep feelings of resentment. In a variety of ways, all children find some outlet for their feelings of resentment.

At this point I want to add a word of caution. Even though your children may be trying to hurt you or get revenge, don't assume their hurtful actions are conscious and willful and can be solved by discipline. Most children who rebel against their parents are hurting because of their unmet, hidden needs. Anger is a way they handle hurts by making others hurt. Condemning your children for their anger or getting mad and fighting back will just perpetuate their feelings of resentment. To help your children resolve their angry feelings, let them talk about the hurts and hidden needs behind their anger. Once they do that, and once you help them meet those needs, their anger will diminish.

The Search for Psychological Safety

Now we come to the final reason children act and feel the way they do. In addition to their inborn temperament, their position in the family, their God-given needs, and the search for revenge, children also have another major motivation. They try to avoid experiencing unhappiness and emotional pain. I call this a search for psychological safety.

Any time children feel unloved, incompetent, unworthy, or bored, they look for substitutes. But they also search for other ways of warding off their uncomfortable feelings. Some children simply *withdraw*. Feeling unloved and fearing rejection, they avoid involvement with the neighborhood children. That way they won't have to suffer more rejection. Or feeling inferior or incompetent, they don't join in neighborhood games. If they don't compete, they can't fail.

Confident parents may have difficulty understanding this type of child. We encourage them to "go out and make some friends," "speak up," or, "be more aggressive." We think, *If*

they don't want to feel lonely, they should get involved. But it is precisely because they feel unloved or lack confidence that they are afraid to get involved. To them it's better to be alone and fear others will reject them than to try to make friends and find out for sure they don't like them! Withdrawal, in other words, provides children with a temporary sense of psychological safety. It is their attempt to make their feelings of loneliness or incompetence more bearable.

Giving up is another way of coping with feelings of incompetence or worthlessness. If you're sure you're going to fail, why try? Many defeated children and teenagers are so afraid of failing again that they just stop trying. This is especially true of depressed children.

Overcompensation is just the opposite of giving up. Some children who don't feel good about themselves throw themselves into their studies or competition or social activities to compensate for their feelings of inferiority or of being unloved. Children who are not naturally good students, for example, may spend hours lifting weights, shooting baskets, running, or in other ways driving themselves in order to excel in athletics. Children who don't feel socially liked and accepted may turn to academics to compensate for their negative self-evaluations.

These teenagers may reach their goals by overcompensation and they may even reap the admiration of their peers or parents. But they can also become very one-sided. The "athlete" can work so hard on his sports that he fails to develop other aspects of his personality. The "scholar" may fail to develop his social life. The "socialite" may neglect his studies. Only years later will they realize what they have missed. And unfortunately, even after these people have excelled in one area they usually continue to feel inadequate in others. Their accolades and achievements provide only temporary relief from their underlying feelings of inferiority and their lack of self-esteem.

Repression is another technique children use to avoid feeling unloved, incompetent, or unworthy. By pushing unpleasant thoughts and feelings about themselves out of awareness, many children try to maintain their emotional equilibrium. Have you noticed, for example, how nearly all young children—let's say up to two or three years of age—tend to be expressive and alert? You don't have to ask a two-year-old how he is feeling; he will spontaneously show his emotions, whether they are positive or negative. But by the time that same child is twenty, he may well be a lot less expressive. He may be less excited over his successes and pleasurable experiences, less able to express dissatisfaction, and less comfortable showing love and feelings of intimacy.

Even by nine or ten, many children learn that "If you say what you are thinking or show your feelings spontaneously, you may be punished or ignored or shamed." So instead of excitedly running to his father with his schoolwork, a young boy simply puts away his books and loses that joyful feeling of sharing with his dad. And instead of telling her mother, "I'm angry at Billy," a girl stuffs her resentment toward her brother because she has been told, "Shame on you. We don't hate our brother. We love our brother." Other children lose touch with their sensitive emotions because they have been told, "Men don't cry," or ridiculed or rejected when they expressed tender emotions. Children need to find acceptable ways to express their strong emotions, but they should not be encouraged to deny or repress those feelings.

Although repression provides a temporary feeling of psychological safety it can cause serious emotional problems later in life. Children who are unable to express their emotions are more likely to develop psychosomatic problems like ulcers, headaches, and lower back pains. They also have difficulties in marriage, where openness and honesty about feelings is important. Sometimes they grow up almost devoid of conscious emotions; they seem more like efficient computers than live, emotional human beings. Others suffer from a loss of

spontaneity or have occasional surprising and destructive out-
bursts of their usually hidden emotions.

You can help your children feel comfortable with their emotions by taking their feelings seriously, listening to them, and
not criticizing or condemning them for their emotions. You
can also help by appropriately expressing your own feelings of
love, joy, excitement, and frustration.

Reaction formation is another unconscious strategy some children use to maintain a sense of psychological safety. In reaction formation, children adopt a conscious attitude that is
exactly the opposite of their true hidden feelings. If a child
has strong feelings of anger, for example, he may become
overtly very loving, kind, and patient, to hide his underlying
hostility. He does this because he feels guilty about his anger
or is afraid he will be punished if he expresses his negative
emotions. But like all mechanisms for finding psychological
safety, reaction formation has its negative side. Children who
are always nice and never angry are a lot like perfectionistic
children who think they must always perform perfectly to be
accepted. Nobody is without some negative emotions—
especially young children. And when children hide their
strong emotions they just increase the likelihood that their
parents and others will overlook their hidden needs.

Rationalization is the last mechanism we will discuss for
providing a sense of psychological safety. In this strategy,
children think up a thousand reasons to explain why they
really aren't at fault or why things are going poorly. If their
team loses, it is because of the umpire. If they receive a low
grade in "conduct," it is because they are sitting next to
someone who "talks all the time." If they fail to finish their
chores, it is because "they had too much to do." The excuses
are endless, but their purpose is consistent. In all ways, at all

costs, they must let someone know that they are innocent and cannot be blamed.

This is a universal human tendency, but I want to look at it from the perspective of your children's hidden needs. Instead of seeing rationalization as simply an attempt to avoid responsibility, remember that your children also turn to rationalization in order to avoid feeling unloved, incompetent, or unworthy. If they acknowledge that they are poor soccer players, for example, they will feel incompetent and inferior. So they blame the referee or some foul play. Other children rationalize their actions or blame others because they know their parents will be angry if they tell the truth. They know it's safer to blame somebody else!

We could list other methods children use to hide their underlying lack of confidence, love, and worth, but this brief survey is enough to show how the process works. Psychologists call these strategies "defense mechanisms" because they defend us from painful or upsetting emotions. I am calling them ways of searching for psychological safety because their major purpose is to ward off uncomfortable inner emotions and provide an inner feeling of psychological safety.

Making It Safe

If you are like most parents, your children's searches for psychological safety can be quite frustrating. A boy who rationalizes every job he fails to do doesn't endear himself to his mom and dad. A teenager who retreats to her room and refuses to talk doesn't make life easy for her parents. In fact, it is easy to react to our children's searches for psychological safety with pressure, anger, or frustration. We may try to force our children to "face the truth," or "speak up" or "come out of their shell," or we may marshall all the evidence to prove they are wrong. But think what that does to a child who is already feeling unloved, incompetent, or unworthy. Being pressured by a stern, eighteen-foot giant only makes them feel more unsafe and misunderstood and want to withdraw or rationalize even more.

The best way to help children give up their safety mechanisms is to help them feel more confident, loved, and worthy. If your son has to blame his team's soccer failures on the referee, don't tell him, "Stop blaming it on the refs. You just blew it." Instead say something like, "That was a tough game, wasn't it?" "It's tough to lose, isn't it?" "You really wanted to win that one, didn't you?" or, "Yes, but you guys played a really good game and you had a great shot [or made a great block] in the second period." And if you want to comment on the referee, you might say, "Yes, that's too bad. It looked like a bad call to me too. But over the course of the season, hopefully those calls will even out."

Comments like these focus in on your son's painful feelings or his needs for confidence—the real sources of his rationalizing. Later, after he has recovered some, you might share your own tendency to "blame the refs" (or your boss or wife!) when you lose. By admitting your feelings of failure, you help your son feel better about his.

Actually your children are probably much like you in their ability to face their failures. Most of us find it easier to admit our weaknesses when we are feeling safe and good about ourselves. But if we know someone is going to blame us or criticize us, we find it harder to be open and honest.

Christian parents have a great example for helping children feel safe. We can can follow God's pattern of dealing with His children. When the apostle John wrote a letter to his fellow

Christians he told them, "My little children, I am writing these things to you that you may not sin. And if anyone sins, we have an Advocate with the Father, Jesus Christ the righteous" (1 John 2:1, 2 NAS). You can sense the tender care in John's voice. He encourages us not to sin but assures us that when we do, we have an advocate. Your children need that type of reassurance and encouragement. They need to see you as their loving advocate who wants them to feel good about themselves, not as a judge who is quick to condemn and pronounce them guilty. As they do, they will feel much safer and not need to turn to the various defense mechanisms in search of psychological safety.

Chapter Highlights

When your children feel unloved, incompetent, or unworthy they turn to the substitutes of attention, power and control, and perfectionism. They may also have one or both of two other reactions. They may become angry and try to get even with the people who haven't helped them feel loved, competent, and worthy, or they may start using a variety of defense mechanisms to provide some psychological safety. A sensitivity to your children's searches for revenge and psychological safety can help tune you in to their hidden needs. Rather than trying to correct or discipline them, you can understand their hurt feelings and take action to meet their underlying needs and address their real problems.

8
Isn't Anything Normal?

By now you may be wondering whether your children ever do anything without some hidden reason or unmet need! Are all their problems caused by the search to fulfill unmet needs, gain revenge, or find psychological safety? Do some problems "just happen" or are they caused by your child's sinful bents or tendencies? That is a good question. Although unmet needs for love, confidence, worth, and activity are a major cause of our children's actions they are not the only one. This chapter and the next look at two other reasons children act and feel the way they do. This chapter discusses some of the everyday problems children have just because they are normal children. Chapter 9 looks at the way sin impacts your children's actions.

The Finicky Eater

A common problem many parents face is getting young children to eat. Some children are born finicky, and most have at least a few strong culinary dislikes. When you couple these picky tastes with a few cups or plates knocked over, a utensil or two sent sailing to the floor, and perhaps an occasional temper tantrum, you can see why mealtime can be one of the most miserable times of the day. In fact in many families the only more conflicting times of the day are bedtime and mornings when you try to get your children up and off to school or church.

To understand why some children don't cooperate at meals, imagine that you are a relatively young infant—perhaps six to ten months of age. For most of your life you have enjoyed either your mother's milk or a satisfying substitute. One day your mother introduces you to another kind of food. Instead of being smooth and liquid, it is soft and mushy. And instead of being body temperature, it is hotter or cooler. It also has an unfamiliar aroma and taste.

If your mother is extremely fortunate, you may like this new experience. But if you are like many children you won't. If you are a Slow-to-Warm-Up Child, for example, your first reaction may be to turn up your nose, pucker your lips, and spit it out! Are you trying to be bad and misbehave? Or are you refusing your mother's offerings because you feel unloved, incompetent, unworthy, or bored? Not at all. You have absolutely no thought of misbehaving and you don't necessarily have any unmet needs. You simply don't like the stuff! You are spitting out something you can't stand.

Your mother, however, doesn't see it this way. She wants you to grow up nice and healthy. She wants you to expand your tastes. And she doesn't want to spend the rest of her life nursing you. Food also has a special meaning for her. For mothers, food equals love. If you accept your mother's food you are accepting her love. If you reject her food you are rejecting her love. Consequently it's very important to your mother that you eat what she puts before you. For these reasons she is going to try everything she can to get you to eat that strange and awful tasting stuff!

If your mother is in a good mood she may smile and play a game like "airplane." She puts a bite on a spoon and with a big sweeping motion gleefully proclaims, "Coming in for a landing." But not to be fooled, you recognize the stuff and spit it out again! Or perhaps your mother decides to use the forceful approach. Since she is bigger than you, she puts a heavy thumb on one side of your jaw and her middle finger on the other and forces you to open up. Then she crams it in. But not to be outdone, you quickly spit it out. Needless to say, this whole scene is hard on everyone concerned.

Other frustrated mothers take the opposite approach. They challenge you, "Okay. If you won't eat it, starve!" With a few refinements that approach is great when children become a little older. But at eight months of age you aren't old enough to understand what she has said, so you go happily on your way, not realizing that your mother is going to refuse to feed you the next time you are hungry. Later, when she does refuse to feed you, you have forgotten the last fiasco and haven't the foggiest notion why she won't give you anything to eat. So you begin to cry.

The best solution is for your parents to recognize that you have limited tastes. Rather than forcing strange-tasting foods down your throat, they could respect your tastes the same way they would like others to respect theirs. They should gradually introduce you to new foods. Can you imagine how you would feel as a grown adult if an eighteen-foot giant stood over you and told you, "I don't care if you like it or not. You are going to sit there until you eat it!" Although you might accommodate yourself to your giant's culinary selections, you would also feel resentful and misunderstood. You weren't misbehaving. After all, you are the one who has to eat it so why not let you decide what's good?

My point is this: Children have limited appetites and we shouldn't force them to eat things they detest. Instead of looking at finicky eating as a sign of rebellion, disobedience, or stubbornness, try to see it for what is is—an entirely normal dislike for certain new foods. And rather than letting the dinner table become a combat zone, try to give your children time to mature and gradually accept new experiences.

This doesn't mean that once your children begin eating solid foods they have the right to demand whatever food they want. If you did that and had four children and a husband you might be fixing five or six different menus for every meal! I suggest that you try to fix at least one dish every family member likes and leave it to them whether or not to eat it. If you have several finicky eaters, you can fix a salad that one of them likes, a main dish that another likes, and a dessert that the other one prefers. This will ensure that no one starves. And once your children learn they can have no snacks unless they have eaten a decent meal, they will begin to broaden their tastes a bit.

"He's Into Everything"

Once children reach the toddler stage, parents encounter a whole new set of problems. Normal, inquisitive toddlers get into everything in sight. Newspapers, magazines, vases, and family heirlooms are all fair game. Like eating problems and mealtime hassles, some parents think these explorations are misbehaviors. They expect their children to leave something alone after they have been told once, and if their children don't, they believe they should be spanked. As one father put it, "A two-year-old must be taught he can't touch things just as we adults can't touch certain things. If he doesn't learn it now he never will."

Although some parents rear their children this way without inflicting any major psychic scars, there is a better way. Like all positive approaches to parenting, this way begins by understanding why your toddlers are continually getting into everything in sight. Once again, try putting yourself in your toddler's shoes. Imagine that you are only a year or so old and are placed in a strange world of people and objects you have never seen. As soon as you are old enough to move around a bit, you want to explore your world. You touch things, put them in your mouth, tear them up, and do everything you can to find out how they work and how they feel. Your inquisitiveness is a healthy sign that you are beginning to use your intelligence and explore your world.

Now imagine that in the middle of your explorations, your eighteen-foot giant comes along, sternly tells you, "No!" and swats your hand. You immediately have a feeling of being bad or doing something wrong. But were you being bad or were you just exploring your world? If you were a couple of years older, your giant's correction would pose no problem since you would understand the necessity of leaving things alone, not breaking Mother's china, or respecting other people's property. But at a year of age you are not mentally capable of comprehending the situation. Consequently you end up feeling confused or bad or angry when your giants spank you. If you are an especially curious child you have an even bigger problem. For twenty years you will be pushing the edge of your parents' limits and trying out every possible experience.

But every move you make will trigger your parents' anxiety and their tendency to label you "bad" instead of simply "curious" or "energetic."

There is an interesting Bible verse that I believe applies to this very situation. It says, "God . . . will not let you be tempted beyond what you can bear. But when you are tempted, he will also provide a way out so that you can stand up under it" (1 Corinthians 10:13). If we look at God as a model parent, this verse is saying that good parents don't tempt their children with more than they can handle. It seems to me that leaving interesting objects within the reach of toddlers is tempting them above what they are able to bear!

Instead of leaving your valuable and breakable objects on the coffee table within your toddler's easy grasp, why not put them on a higher shelf or table? Kiddie-proof your home. By the time your children reach three years of age or so they will understand why they should leave things alone. Then you can put the objects back and discipline your children when they get into things they shouldn't. In the meantime, don't tempt them beyond what they can bear. And if you must have a few forbidden items within their reach, be sure you not only tell them what they cannot play with, but also give them a way out by showing them interesting substitutes or turning their attention to other things.

Surviving Shopping With Your Children

If mealtimes are some of the most frustrating times inside the home, shopping trips have to be among the most frustrating times outside the house. If your young children are normal, they will probably start asking for things the moment you walk into the store. They will run throughout the store, take things off the shelves, push the shopping cart wildly down the aisle, throw a tantrum when they can't have their way, or create some other kind of disturbance. Once again, are these children trying to make life miserable for you or acting out of an unmet need? Not necessarily. Like mealtime hassles and knocking over your knickknacks, this kind of behavior is often more of a normal action than a misbehavior.

Imagine walking into a huge store with your giant parent. You are intrigued with the array of interesting things—many of which you have seen on television. As you walk up and

down the aisles, your giant parent takes one thing after another off the shelves and puts them into her cart. Everything she wants, she gets. But the moment you point or ask or grab for something she tells you no and keeps on going. Before long, this gets a little frustrating. You have nothing to do, can make no choices, and you have to watch your eighteen-foot giant get everything she wishes. What normal child wouldn't get a little tired of this?

As a parent, you can avoid this upsetting situation by finding ways to involve your children in the shopping. If they are old enough, send them off to pick up a few items on your list. Don't send them after the eggs or some other breakable item. But they can certainly pick up the toilet paper or a can of beans without causing too much damage! You can also let them select an item or two of their own preference. If you need dry cereal, for example, let them select one variety. I realize they will choose whatever they have seen advertised lately, and it will probably be multicolored and contain a prize. But if you can stand it, let them. You can also ask them to bring you one of your old standbys like corn flakes or oatmeal.

Another helpful tactic is to allow your children to pick out one toy or one piece of candy to hold their interest while you are shopping. You can either let them do this early or hold it as a reward for good behavior and let them pick it up at the checkout stand. Although some parents think it is spoiling children to get something every time they go shopping, realize that that is exactly what *we* do when we enter a store. We fill several large bags with things we want and think we spoil our children if we buy them a little piece of candy! Maybe our children deserve the same privilege we have on a much more limited scale.

Out of Bed and Off to School

Once your children are old enough for school, you have another set of problems. How can you get them up and out of bed and off to school without suffering a nervous breakdown? Left to themselves, children tend to sleep in, fuss, dawdle, forget their chores, and miss the bus or car pool every morning. They put things off until about three minutes before they should be out the door and then call for help in panic. Like finicky eating and problems in the market, this kind of problem usually isn't the result of unmet emotional needs. Your children don't forget to make their beds, brush their teeth, feed the dog, or get out of the shower because they feel unloved, incompetent, unworthy, or bored. It's just human nature. Very few children seem to be born with the desire to make their beds and be neat and on time!

When our children were young we faced this problem. From the time Kathy and I were up in the mornings, we spent most of our time checking on Dickie and Debbie's progress. We glanced in their rooms to see if their beds were made. We checked the bathroom to see if they had been there. And we asked if they had brushed their teeth, washed their faces, combed their hair, set the table, practiced the piano, and finished a number of other daily duties.

Finally we tired of this routine and decided to find a better way. We began by establishing a morning routine. Rather than having our children get up around 7:00, eat sometime between 7:15 and 7:45, and practice piano whenever they could, we developed a daily schedule for Dickie and Debbie. Everyone was up by 7:00. By 7:30 the prebreakfast chores had to be done and one of the children had the table set. Promptly at 7:30 we sat down for breakfast. At 7:45 one of the children cleared the table while the other practiced the piano for fifteen minutes. And in the remaining fifteen or twenty minutes before leaving for school, other morning activities were finished.

We also built a little "job box" that held a variety of colored three-by-five cards. Each card had one morning activity printed in bold letters. Dickie and Debbie each had a job box that was divided into two sections. One was marked TO DO; the other read DONE. Every morning before sitting down for breakfast, each child had to check his or her box and see that all of the prebreakfast chores were finished. Before they left for school, they had to be sure the remainder were done. This simple little box had a profound effect. It let us stop nagging and helped our children accept responsibility for their own morning activities. Instead of relying on us to remind them a dozen times, they simply checked their own job boxes.

That planning helped turn a potentially bad situation into a very good one. Without our leadership and structure, Dickie and Debbie were wandering from one thing to another. They didn't know just when to count on breakfast and they didn't have the help of their job box to remind them of undone chores.

Simple steps like this are an important part of parenting. Although you don't need to develop a rigid program for all your children's activities, nearly all children need some help planning their schedules and deciding when and how to carry out their regular responsibilities. On top of bringing order into your family, this initiates good habits that will last a lifetime.

Chapter Highlights

Not all of your children's problems and misbehaviors are caused by trying to fulfill some God-given needs by turning to a substitute or counterfeit. Many everyday problems are simply the normal results of being a child. Instead of seeking out your children's hidden needs to solve these problems, you need to look at their obvious needs—the need for training, the need for a little structure and help with their schedules, the need to feel involved in shopping, the need for a good example, and perhaps the need for some clear consequences or discipline for chores that are left undone.

When a young child leaves his room in a chaotic condition simply because of the natural human tendency to put off anything that smacks of work, you don't need to take a lot of time to play with that child and communicate your love to him. You can move right in and help him find some ways of organizing his time and life. He probably just needs a little training and direction in order to carry out his responsibilities.

9
Your Child and Adam

A couple of years ago I was asked to speak to the parents of a Christian elementary school on the topic "Why Children Misbehave." The PTA had plastered posters with my picture and the title of my talk around campus and announced the meeting in all the students' classes. On the day of my talk, one of the fifth graders walked up to the principal and asked, "Why do we need that guy to tell us why we misbehave? We already know that. It's because we're sinners."

In spite of the boy's confident assurance that parents didn't need a psychologist telling them why their children misbehave, the principal went ahead with the meeting. But actually the boy had raised a good question. The Bible does say all problems stem ultimately from sin. It's not enough to attribute all of our children's misbehaviors to their inborn temperaments or their unmet needs for love, confidence, and worth. To properly understand our children's misbehaviors we must also understand the role sin plays in their lives. On the other hand, to simply label our children's problems "sin" and go on as though that explains everything also misses the point. We must ask ourselves, *How does sin cause my children's problems?* or *Why does my children's sinfulness show up in this particular type of problem?*

According to the Bible, sin impacts our children's lives in at least two ways. First, through the sins and imperfections of others—such as parents, siblings, friends, and teachers. Once Adam and Eve decided to take matters into their own hands and rebel against God, their sin was immediately passed on to others in their family (Genesis 3:5). Adam and Eve blamed each other and they undoubtedly started having their share of family quarrels (Genesis 3:11–13). Their children, Cain and Abel, experienced the first case of sibling rivalry—one that eventually ended in murder (Genesis 4:1–10).

Since Adam and Eve, there have been no perfect parents. No matter how well-intended, we parents have problems of our own. We can be so anxious, critical, or controlling that we undermine our children's needs for confidence. We can be so involved in our own activities that we ignore our children's needs for love. We can speak harshly or punish our children in ways that attack their sense of worth. In short, our sinfulness and our problems can be communicated to our children through our failure to fulfill their God-given needs. When children misbehave because these God-given needs have not been met we can say they are misbehaving because of *others'* sins—usually their parents, teachers, or their peers.

This, however, is only one side of the coin. According to the Bible your children would have problems even if you were a perfect parent. Adam and Eve couldn't blame their problems on their parent. They didn't rebel against God and try to prove they were powerful because their needs for confidence weren't met. He had put them in charge of the earth. They didn't feel inferior because God had criticized them or belittled them; He had pronounced them very good. And they certainly didn't sin because they were bored. He had instructed them to rule over the earth as His appointed caretakers! Yet in spite of this, Adam and Eve still decided to challenge God's authority and be their own bosses. Their sins were clearly their own responsibility.

Let's say the situation was different. What if God had placed Adam and Eve in the Garden, created them with a necessity to eat in order to survive, placed only one source of food in the Garden (the tree of the knowledge of good and evil), and told them if they ate that fruit they would die. Perhaps Adam and Eve would have been able to comply with God's direction for a while. But in time they would have to eat or starve to death. In that scenario, who would be to blame for Adam and Eve's sin? Wouldn't we have to say that it was God? He would have created them with the necessity of eating to survive but failed to make any provision for their need. That would obviously be cruel. Yet this is precisely what some parents do. They bring children into the world and then busy themselves with so many other things that their children feel left out and ignored. Then, when their children get into trouble to force their parents to give them some attention, the parents blame their children for the problems!

God did just the opposite. He created both a man and a woman so they could meet each other's needs for love. He filled the Garden with attractive fruit to meet their needs for food. He gifted them and gave them plenty to do to keep them occupied. And He let them know how significant they were to Him. Then, since He had fully met their needs, they had to accept the full responsibility for their sins. Unfortu-

nately we can't say the same thing of our children. Part of
every child's problem has at least a little to do with his or her
parent's imperfections.

Everyone Wants to Be Number One

When Adam and Eve sinned, it was because they wanted to
"be like God, knowing good and evil" (Genesis 3:5). In other
words, they wanted to run their own lives and they didn't
want to play second fiddle to anyone—including God. I believe this is the essence of our own and our children's personal
sin. Everyone wants to be number one.

If you've watched your children's soccer or baseball games
or other competition you know what I mean. No children go
out there thinking, *Boy, we love to lose!* or even, *We'd just like
to tie.* They want to win. They want to be the best. If they
win, they run excitedly off the field with a certain air of confidence. But if they lose, they walk slowly off the field, defeated and rejected. Some children lack confidence so much
they give up and don't try anymore.

If you have more than one child, you have undoubtedly
seen them compete for your love and attempt to be number
one in your life. I remember years ago when our son, Dickie,
popped into my lap and asked, "Daddy, do you love me?"

"*I sure do,*" I replied, giving him a big hug.

"How much?" Dickie queried.

"As much as any father has ever loved a son, Dickie," I
answered, looking him straight in the eye.

"Really?" Dickie responded with a big smile.

"Really!" I replied. Then, with a mischievous look on his
face, he asked, "More than Debbie?"

I thought fast and answered, "Dickie, you are our first child and our son, and I have a very special love for you!"

"Really?" he responded as he lit up again.

"Really!" I replied.

Then he asked again, "More than Debbie?"

"Dickie," I replied, "Debbie is our second child and our daughter, and I have a very special kind of love for her."

"Oh," he said, as a discouraged look spread over his face.

Round and round we went with Dickie trying every way he knew to con me into telling him I loved him more than Debbie! My assurances that I loved him with all the love I had, that I loved him with a special love, and that I didn't love anyone more than him wouldn't really satisfy him. He wanted to be number one!

All children have similar desires. They aren't content simply being loved; they want to be loved more than anyone else. They aren't content being average, healthy, competent people; they would like to be more competent or powerful than others. They aren't satisfied with just a healthy sense of worth; they would like to be better or more important than others. And they aren't content to busy themselves simply with what God intended; they would like to do whatever they please!

This shows up at school, at home, and in their social lives. It influences the way they dress, the way they act, and the way they get along with others. While not every child competes in every field, most children try to find one or more areas where they can be "the best." In fact, have you noticed that children in the same family often tend to find their identity in different activities so they won't have to compete head-to-head with their brothers and sisters? If your first child is a gifted athlete, your second might become a serious student and the third a socialite. One might even decide to be the

family rebel! Each one of your children tries to choose an identity in which he or she can "be the best"—at least in their own family.

Around the house, the desire to be number one often shows up in putting down one's brothers and sisters. Although sibling conflicts are accentuated by parental favoritism, criticism, lack of clearly communicated love, and unwise comparisons, these are not the sole causes. Even in loving homes with sensitive parents, there will be some sibling fights. These fights are usually caused by the desire of one child to be either the most loved or the most competent. By beating up their brother or sister, your sons and daughters attempt to feel more confident. And by being so nice that you favor them, they try to be the most loved.

The desire to do one's best isn't bad. That is actually a gift from God. It is only when we shift our goal from doing *our* best to beating others that problems come. In every match there is a winner and a loser. The winner earns good feelings about himself by defeating the loser—not simply by doing his best. The Bible gives a perfect antidote to this. It tells us, "Let everyone be sure that he is doing his very best, for then he will have the personal satisfaction of work well done, and won't need to compare himself with someone else" (Galatians 6:4 TLB).

Shared Responsibility

Most of your children's misbehaviors grow out of a mixture of their search to fulfill unmet needs and their own sinful tendencies. Take a child who becomes extremely bossy or controlling and demanding. Some of this is just his fallen human nature. He wants to be number one. Most of us would like to be in charge if we had the opportunity, and few of us like others telling us how to run our lives. But this innate desire to run our own lives is only part of the picture. Children who feel especially inferior or weak because they have been repeatedly compared with others or criticized can become exceptionally stubborn and controlling to compensate for their unmet need for confidence. These two influences work together to shape the stubborn child's behavior.

Consider a promiscuous teenage boy or girl. These adolescents are often using repeated sexual encounters to search for the love they don't experience at home. To that degree, their parents' failure to communicate their love is a good part of the problem. The promiscuous teenagers are turning to premarital sex to gain attention as a substitute for their God-given need for love. But these teenagers must also take some responsibility for their own behavior. There are other ways of meeting their needs for love rather than giving in to their sexual urges or the pressures of their peers. And some teenagers become sexually active for the physical thrill of it, not because they feel unloved at home.

Or think about a twenty-year-old Christian girl who marries a non-Christian against the advice of her parents and the Bible's teachings. It would be one thing if that girl were a happy, well-adjusted young woman who was convinced of her parents' love but just decided to ignore the Bible's teachings. But what if she had been abused or ignored at home so that she felt worthless and unloved and was vulnerable to the first man who treated her with deep love and respect? In the latter case, wouldn't we have to say her parents share in the responsibility for her poor decision? If she wasn't so starved for love, she would find it a lot easier to wait for a Christian husband.

The delicate interaction of your children's desires to be number one and your responsibility to successfully meet their God-given needs for love, confidence, and worth calls for a lot of sensitivity on your part. You need to be sensitive to both your children's sinful tendencies and their needs for love, confidence, and worth. You need to learn the difference between sibling fights caused by your lack of attention to your children or their boredom and those growing out of their natural wish to beat up on their brother or sister!

If you take all of the responsibility for your children's problems, you will end up feeling guilty, angry, or depressed. But

if you blame all of your children's problems on them, you will
miss their God-given needs for love and confidence and worth,
and program them for anger, discouragement, or depression.
In reality there is probably never a time that your children's
actions (or your own for that matter) aren't influenced both by
their sinful tendencies and their less-than-perfect parents. I
know that is true for my children. Even though I have loved
them deeply and tried to meet their needs, I was not a perfect
parent. Consequently I have to take some responsibilities for
their problems.

Two Ways of Discipline

The way we discipline our children should be influenced by
our judgment of whether their behaviors are stemming largely
from their own sinful tendencies, their inherited temperaments, their normal childish reactions, or our failures to help
them feel loved, confident, and worthy. Take, for example, a
child who is misbehaving or fighting with his brother to gain
attention because he feels unloved. If we spank him or send
him to his room he may stop his misbehavior. But what have
we done to meet his need for love? We have actually punished
him for being unable to clearly tell us he needs our love. Even
if he behaves the way we want him to, he will continue feeling lonely, unloved, or depressed. On top of that, he may feel
worse because he has been punished for trying to meet a
God-given need.

Think how differently that boy would feel if we recognize
his misbehavior as a symptom of a hidden need. What if
instead of sending him to his room we asked, "Billy, do you
know why you keep picking on your brother?" or said, "Billy,
you don't seem to be feeling very good today." Once we had

his attention, we might sensitively say, "I wonder if you're feeling bad because you want Mommy to spend more time with you?" or, "I wonder if you think Mommy spends too much time with Johnnie?" or, "I wonder if you want Mommy to pay more attention to you?"

When you get close to the truth, you will usually see a little smile of recognition on your son's face. He will know that you understand his hidden message and start feeling better quickly! Then, once you understand what your son is trying to tell you by his behavior, you can help him find better ways to meet those needs. You might set aside more time to talk with him about his day's activities, or to play together. Or you might work on showing more physical affection or communicating your love in clearer ways. And you can teach your children better ways of telling you when they are feeling left out or lonely rather than starting a fight.

When my children were very young, they learned to come to us and say, "Daddy [or Mommy], I need a little more attention." You can't believe how rewarding it is to see your child come up with a questioning smile and tell you his needs like that. You can sense his trust in you, his knowledge that you really want his best, and his assurance that if he tells you what he needs, you will do your best to help. You also know that in his coming to you, he has probably chosen not to try to gain attention by beating on his sister or some other unacceptable means.

In much the same way, if your daughter is acting stubborn and uncooperative because she is feeling inferior or incompetent, you might say something like, "It seems as if you really want your way!", "You really don't want anyone telling you what to do today, do you?" or, "It seems like you really want to show Dad you're the boss!" Once again, when you see a sign of recognition on her face, you will know you are on the right track. Then you can set out some ways of building up her confidence.

If the problem is rooted in your children's search for psychological safety, you can say something like, "It really seems scary out there, doesn't it?" or, "It's really hard to be wrong, isn't it?" or, "You must not feel too happy down inside." All these comments get into your children's shoes and let them know you understand that they don't feel safe. Then you can encourage them to tell you more about how they are feeling. The more you understand their frightening inner world, the better you can help them to develop the confidence and skills they need to give up their maladaptive safety measures.

In each case your goal is to become your children's friend or ally in order to help them meet their needs. That is the key ingredient of positive parenting. This approach initially takes a little time and effort. But with practice you can learn to be sensitive to the needs and feelings that lie beneath your children's misbehavior. When you do, you will be in a much better position to discipline and train effectively.

Once your children's needs are met, you can apply the usual techniques of discipline. Sending them to their rooms, missing a meal, staying inside, or skipping television can all be appropriate techniques of discipline. But if we apply these techniques without also attending to our children's needs we do them a great disservice.

Parents who focus solely on their children's behavior are missing the essence of their sons' and daughters' personalities. The Bible says, "Out of the overflow of the heart the mouth speaks" (Matthew 12:34). In other words, God's first concern is our inner attitudes and feelings. When these are in good shape, healthy behaviors will follow naturally. This is as true of children as of adults. No amount of forcing, pressuring, or molding your children's actions will be sufficient to make them healthy. They will only mature as they feel increasingly loved, competent, and worthy. You can train a dog or other animal by simply shaping their behavior. But human beings aren't just animals. They have feelings and needs and wishes and desires. In order to grow up happily they must have those needs understood and met.

Here are some questions that can help you tell when your children are misbehaving because they want to be number one, when they are motivated by a search to find substitutes for unmet needs, and when their reactions are normal "childishness." These guidelines aren't absolute, and nearly all problems have a little of each. But they can help you sense the primary source of some of your children's actions.

- Do most children your child's age tend to act the way he does? (If so, it's more likely that the behavior or attitude is a natural, childish behavior than an unmet need or a sinful tendency.)
- Has your child tended to be this way from early in life? (If so, it's more likely that the behavior is his or her inborn temperament.)
- Have you done anything today to help your children feel loved, accepted, and an integral part of your family? (If you have, it's more likely their misbehaviors are caused by their own sinful or naturally childish tendencies.)
- Are you and your spouse good at freely expressing your affection for each other and for your children? (If so, it's more likely their misbehaviors stem from their own sinful or naturally childish tendencies.)

- Are you and your spouse good at complimenting and encouraging your children and helping them feel confident? (If so, it's more likely their misbehaviors stem from their own sinful or naturally childish tendencies.)
- Do you or your spouse tend to be overly anxious or critical or controlling? (If so, it's more likely their misbehaviors stem from your difficulty in helping them meet their God-given needs.)
- Has anything happened recently that would undermine your children's confidence? (If so, it's more likely their actions are coming from unmet needs.)
- Have your children been active in constructive, interesting activities? (If so, it is more likely that their behavior is caused by their own sinful or naturally childish tendencies.)
- Are your children feeling good about themselves? (If they are, it is more likely that their problems stem from their own sinful tendencies.)
- Is the atmosphere in your family generally happy and cooperative with only sporadic problems? (If it is, it's more likely that your children's problems come from their own sinful or naturally childish tendencies.)
- Do you lose your temper with your children a lot and punish or speak to them in angry words and tones? (If so, it's more likely some of their misbehaviors are stemming from your difficulty in helping them meet their God-given needs.)

Chapter Highlights

Children don't misbehave simply because of their inborn temperaments or because they are trying to fill their unmet needs for love, confidence, and worth by turning to their substitutes. They also misbehave because all human beings tend to want to run their own lives and be number one. These varied causes of your children's misbehaviors have important implications for successful parenting. To discipline your children effectively you need to sense when their actions are largely caused by your failure to meet their God-given needs and when they are caused by their own sinful tendencies or directions.

10
Finding Your Child's Hidden Needs

By now you may be saying, "That's fine for you, but I'm not a psychologist. I can't take all day to analyze the reasons my children act the way they do. It's all I can handle just to tell them to shape up and punish them when they don't."

I know how you feel; sometimes I feel the same way! But the fact is, focusing on your children's behavior is at best a temporary solution. Even when discipline produces the behavior change you desire, it doesn't fill your children's inner needs for love and confidence and worth. They will simply act up again later to try to find a substitute fulfillment or push their needs underground and develop serious long-term personal problems.

Fortunately, it really isn't difficult to tune in to your children's major emotional needs. All you need to look at is one or more of these things: (1) your children's behavior, (2) your feelings when your children misbehave, and (3) your children's response to your attempt to correct them.

Think about your children's behavior for a minute. It will give you a very good idea of their hidden needs. If your daughter is constantly interrupting you or getting into trouble, she must either be looking for attention because she feels neglected and unloved or looking for some destructive activity to ward off her boredom. If your son is being stubborn or defiant, he must be trying to gain power and control to ward off his feelings of smallness, weakness, and incompetence. If your daughter is constantly perfectionistic, she is probably hiding some underlying lack of sense of worth. And if your son is often angry and resentful, he must be wanting to get revenge on you or others whom he feels have failed to meet his needs for love, confidence, or worth. Each need results in some predictable types of misbehavior. Table I shows how each of your children's misbehaviors points toward a specific unmet emotional need.[1]

The second easy way to recognize your children's hidden needs is to monitor your own feelings when your children misbehave. If you are feeling bothered and annoyed because your children keep on interfering with your work or getting into trouble, why do you think you are feeling that way? Chances are you are feeling bothered because your children *want* you to feel bothered because they are feeling left out, alone, or bored. In other words, you can tell when your children are interrupting you or misbehaving because they feel bored or need your attention because you will feel bothered or annoyed.

If you react to your children's misbehaviors by feeling an-

---

[1] The format of the three tables in this chapter is adapted from *Winning Children Over* by Francis X. Walton and Robert L. Powers (Chicago: The American Institute of Adlerian Studies, Ltd., 1974; 1990). Used by permission.

Table I

Our Child's Behavior

If our child's motivation is . . . he will probably be	
Attention	Noisy, restless, a showoff, and getting into situations that guarantee we will stop what we are doing and focus on him.
Power and control	Aggressive, defiant toward authority, insolent, and will refuse to do his work, disobey, try to be the boss, and pout and sulk when he cannot have his way. May also use passive control methods.
Perfectionism and performance	Extremely polite and cooperative. A good student who tries very hard to please. May also show signs of pressure and disappointment when he cannot be the best.
Destructive activity	Bored, restless, goes from one thing to another, frequently interrupts and asks, "What can I do?" or gets into some mischievous or destructive activity.
Revenge	Verbally or physically assaultive or hurtful, teasing.
Psychological safety	Avoiding situations and feelings that are potentially threatening, or trying to ensure his innocence or safety. May give up and stop trying.

gry, challenged, and defeated, chances are they are not looking for love. Your feelings of being challenged tell you they are trying to gain power or control by resisting you. It's a sure sign they are attempting to overcome their feelings of smallness, inadequacy, or incompetency.

And what if you feel proud of your child but are afraid she might be under too much pressure and unable to relax? That's a good sign she might be turning to perfectionism to hide her concerns about her basic sense of worth or value as a person. Table II summarizes the ways your feelings can help you see your children's hidden needs.

Table II

Our Reaction to Our Child's Misbehavior

If our child's motivation is . . . we will probably feel	
Attention	Annoyed and tend to think of our child as a pest or a bother. He is in the way or disturbing us.
Power and control	Angry, challenged, or defeated. We will want to fight back to prove we are the boss, or give up and quit.
Perfectionism	Pride in our child but wonder if he is "too good." We may be concerned about his inability to relax, take it easy, or not always be "the winner."
Destructive activity	Bothered and want to be left alone. We think they should find ways of taking care of themselves.
Revenge	Angry or, if the child is older, hurt. How could they treat us this way after all we have done for them?
Psychological safety	Frustrated because we don't know how to reach our child. Other reactions vary with our child's defense. In withdrawal we may feel like giving up or be very worried. In rationalization we may become angry.

If your children's behavior and your own reactions to your children aren't enough to lead you to their needs, there is one more set of signals. That is your children's reactions to your attempts at discipline. If your children are misbehaving to gain attention because they feel unloved or ignored, for example, they will probably temporarily stop their misbehaviors when you discipline them. Since they got your attention by misbehaving they will be fine for a while. But the next time they feel left out or unloved they will misbehave again to get some more attention. Consequently, if your children repeatedly go through a cycle of misbehaving, then doing better when you discipline them, but soon misbehave again, that's a good sign their needs for love aren't being fully met. Table III shows how your children's response to discipline can point to their hidden needs.

Table III

Our Child's Response to Discipline

If our child's motivation is . . . he will probably respond to correction by	
Attention	Stopping for a short time (because he received more attention) but then beginning again (since he is looking for more).
Power and control	Continuing to fight in some way. He may get worse, threaten retaliation, or find a passive means of control.
Perfectionism and performance	Trying harder, becoming discouraged, or feeling he can't please.
Destructive activity	Feeling misunderstood, becoming discouraged, or continuing to seek for some way to break the boredom.
Revenge	Talking back, becoming worse, or seeking other means of retaliating.
Psychological safety	Increasing his use of the mechanisms already in use.

God's Part and Ours

Near the end of his letter to the church at Philippi, the apostle Paul wrote these words: "And my God shall supply all your needs according to His riches in glory in Christ Jesus" (Philippians 4:19 NAS).

Taken by themselves, Paul's words seem to imply that God will somehow miraculously meet all of His children's needs. But if you go back through the first three chapters of his letter to the Philippians you notice an interesting thing. Paul began by telling the Christians at Philippi how much he loved them and missed them and how important their joint work for Christ had been. Then he spent most of three chapters encouraging the Christians to get along with one another and telling them how they could serve and help one another grow. He encouraged them to "be of the same mind," to "maintain the same love," to be "united in spirit," to regard others as more important than themselves, and to have the same attitude that Christ had toward them—an attitude of loving service.

God certainly loves His children and communicates His love for us. But according to Paul it was through the loving, supportive relationships with other members of the family of God that God was going to meet the needs of the Christians at Philippi.

The same thing is true of our children. God loves our children and promises to meet their needs but He doesn't do it miraculously or without our help. He has given us the wonderful opportunity to put ourselves in our children's shoes and learning to sense their hidden needs. Then, as His representatives here on earth, God asks us to take the time to help them feel like the gifted, loved, and important people they are to Him and to us. One of the greatest gifts you can give to your children is the time and commitment to understand their needs for love and confidence and worth and help them meet them. As you do, you will be preparing them for a lifetime of good feelings about themselves and for meaningful and healthy relationships with others. You will also cut down on a very significant percentage of their daily misbehaviors.

Part IV
Exercises for
Growing Parents

11
What Do We Do Next?

I have some friends who are fantastic parents. Carl and Brenda are naturally cool, calm, and collected. They enjoy their children, have a lot of energy, and are sensitive and kind. They also find it easy to set reasonable limits and calmly discipline their children when they need it. Even when their children reached adolescence, things continued to go smoothly. They enjoyed their teenagers and their friends, took an interest in their activities, and just seemed to like rearing teenagers. They enjoyed talking with their adolescents about their activities and had a way of drawing them out when they were feeling upset. They also knew how to say no in ways their teenagers could accept. As far as I know, Carl and Brenda never read a book on parenting and never asked for any advice on raising happy children. They were just naturally effective parents.

Most of us aren't that way. In fact, I envy Carl and Brenda. As young parents, my wife and I both tended to lose our tempers with our children and found it easier to try to pressure

them into behavioral conformity than to sensitively understand
their needs. We had to put in a lot of time and effort to become
effective parents. I suspect most parents are the same way. In
fact, most of us need to do more than read a book or get some
good advice. We need to develop some new habits and better
ways of relating to our children. Most of us also need some practice to understand our children's needs and find the best ways
of dealing with their problems and misbehaviors. Because of
that, I have put together a series of exercises designed to help
you apply the concepts of this book. These exercises make up
the rest of Part IV of *Your Child's Hidden Needs.*

Each chapter in Part IV begins with a brief review of the
key points of one of the chapters from Parts I, II, and III.
Then it gives you a set of exercises to help you apply those
concepts in your own family.

These application chapters are written so you can use them
in a study group or a class as well as by yourself. Each chapter
can easily be completed in less than an hour. If at all possible,
I encourage you to do them with your spouse or a few friends.
Discussing your children with others is usually a better way of
learning than doing things by yourself. If you use this book in
a study group, I suggest that you study one chapter during
each meeting. If you go much faster than this, you probably
won't have enough time to apply the principles to your family
life. If you go much slower than one chapter each month you
will tend to forget what you have learned earlier.

If You Are in a Study Group

Now let's assume you'd like to be in a study group. Your
first thought may well be, *Who would be our leader?* Let me
suggest that you might be the perfect person! You don't have

to be an expert to lead this workbook study. In fact, these exercises aren't written to be "taught." They are intended to be practiced and experienced. All you need is a desire to be a better parent, an ability to get along with others, and a willingness to do a little work. Then merely talk to a few friends; if they're interested, you're on your way.

Here are some suggestions for your first meeting. After that the basic pattern is established.

1. Begin by having the members introduce themselves and tell one unique or humorous quality about one of their children. It is also good to ask members why they came to the study group and what they hope to gain from it.

2. See that each person has a copy of this book.

3. List the topics to be covered at each meeting and assign the chapter to be read each week. I suggest that you follow the sequence of chapters used in the book because the order was established with a study group in mind.

4. Use approximately fifteen minutes of the meeting for reading chapter 1. It is not a lengthy chapter, and most people will read it within fifteen minutes; besides, this eliminates the need to lecture! After everyone has finished, take a few minutes to review the basic ideas. Then have everyone fill out exercise 1 in the first workbook chapter. This, too, should take no more than ten or fifteen minutes. In two simple steps you have involved everyone in the class activities. Sharing answers to exercise 1 is a good way to close the first session.

5. Arrange to phone each member once a week or have group members select a phone partner or phone cou-

ple. Phone partners help remind each other to do their homework and pray and help each other with their children.

After the first session you are well on your way. The exercises will carry the group along step by step, and the only input you need to give is to moderate the group discussions. Here are a few pointers for guiding those discussions.

1. Encourage everyone to participate by calling on the more quiet persons to share their answers. I often ask each person in the group to relate her or his answer to one of the exercises.
2. Encourage members to share specific examples of their successes and failures. The successes encourage others, and the failures provide an opportunity to clarify things when techniques are being misapplied.
3. Be positive and complimentary when members are sharing.
4. After someone describes an attempt to apply a new principle, explore how successfully it worked. Encourage members to point out effective techniques and positive attitudes. Also see that they kindly but clearly mention weaknesses in the applications.
5. If one person tries to dominate the conversation, express thanks for their comments and then say something like, "Now, I'd like to know what Bill has tried."
6. Encourage members to share relevant Scripture passages and principles.
7. Use the first few minutes of each meeting to briefly review the major points of the previous lesson.

8. Use the next portion of each meeting to discuss attempts to apply the previous lesson's principles. Here is a good chance to have each person share one experience.

9. If you decide not to present the new material in a lecture, simply make the reading assignment for the next meeting and close. If you meet for longer than one hour, it is often good to use twenty or thirty minutes at the close of each meeting for reading the next chapter and completing one of the workbook exercises. There are two reasons for this working ahead. First, most of us are busy, and second, we don't read much. You may get some people to read more during that twenty or thirty minutes than they would during the rest of the entire week! When you introduce each new lesson in this way, you see that everyone gets started. The personal satisfaction that comes from beginning a new lesson encourages everyone to complete the work for the next meeting.

10. Establish the following principle: Anyone can share an experience or give an opinion on the part of the lesson being discussed as long as he or she has done the preliminaries of reading that part of the chapter and completing the workbook exercise. There are important reasons for this. Some people like to talk excessively about their own ideas. By seeing to it that everyone who talks has read the material and completed the exercise, the tendency to stray is radically reduced. This restriction also indicates to the members the importance of applying the material, and it motivates them to do the work.

An Ounce of Prevention *Is* Worth a Pound of Cure!

Many parents follow a "fire engine approach" to parenting. We go from one crisis or emergency to the next, constantly putting out fires or solving problems after they are well under way.

This all-too-common pattern robs both our children and ourselves of much joy and fulfillment God intends for us in family living. It can also be the seedbed for serious problems in the future. In fact, many of Satan's major victories are won right here in the home! This doesn't have to be.

In these exercises we will be practicing an alternative method of parenting. These exercises focus on the positive side of parenting and on ways of meeting our children's needs and solving problems *before* they happen. Some parents find this comes naturally, but most of us have to break out of some old habits and learn new ways of understanding and guiding our children if we are going to parent positively. This first workbook chapter is written to help you focus on some of the

problems or areas of concern you may want to work on with
your children. The exercise chapters that follow will help you
develop a specific plan for solving these problems and meeting your children's hidden needs.

Exercise 1

Discuss with your spouse or study group several of the frus-
trations (small or large) you experience as a parent (e.g., constant interruptions, not listening, sibling fights, curfew
problems, sassiness, alcohol or drugs, disobedience, etc.).

A. List three of these problem behaviors you would most like
   to change.

   1. _____

   2. _____

   3. _____

B. What effect do the conflicts and concerns you mentioned
   above have on your life? In other words, how do you feel
   about them and what do they do to your peace and enjoyment in life?_____

   _____

   _____

   _____

   _____

C. How do you typically handle these problems or react to
   them (e.g., become angry, withdraw, give up, go to work
   and get away from it all, etc.)?_____

_____

_____

_____

_____

_____

D. How do your children respond to the reaction you mentioned above?_____

_____

_____

_____

_____

_____

E. If you could find ways of eliminating even half of these problems, how do you think you would feel, and how might it change your personal and family life?

_____

_____

_____

_____

Exercise 2

Our styles of discipline and family living are usually influenced by the way our own parents reared us. We either tend to rear our children like one (or both) of our parents reared us or to do just the opposite!

A. Describe your parents' style of child rearing. Give special attention to their methods of discipline and their attitudes and emotional reactions to your misbehavior. (For example, were they strict, permissive, or balanced? Were they rather distant and uninvolved, or were they warm and close? Were they the nagging type? Did they threaten or yell a lot? Did they instruct you lovingly and clearly? Did they utilize physical spanking?)

_____

_____

_____

_____

_____

_____

B. How are your child-rearing practices similar to or different from your parents? Give an example or two to illustrate.

_____

_____

_____

_____

_____

_____

Exercise 3

One of our goals in this study is to learn to replace some of the everyday conflicts we so often encounter with fun, relaxed, and enjoyable family experiences.

A. Think of one of the happiest, fulfilling, or meaningful times you experienced as a child with your parents and describe it below. Tell what you were doing, how you and your parents felt, and why it was such a great time.

_____

_____

_____

_____

_____

B. As you think back on that experience, why do you think it went so well? In other words, what was going on in your life or in your parents' lives that allowed you to have such a good time? List several specific things that probably helped that day go so well (e.g., your parents were not tired; you were so busy you didn't have time to fight; your parents had planned activities everyone would enjoy, etc.).

_____

_____

_____

_____

_____

_____

_____

C. Think of one of the happiest times you have experienced with one or more of your own children and describe that experience below. Give special attention to how you and your children felt._____

_____

_____

_____

_____

_____

_____

D. Why do you think that time went so well? In other words, what was going on in your life or your spouse's or children's lives that allowed such good things to happen?

_____

_____

_____

_____

_____

Exercise 4

Christian parents can learn a great deal about parenting by looking at God's relationship with His earthly children as a model or example of how we can relate to our own children.

A. Brainstorm (with your spouse or study group) on as many of the positive, preventive aspects of God's relationship with us as you can think of. Then list these below and give specific scriptural references that illustrate each.

1. _____

2. _____

3. _____

4. _____

5. _____

6. _____

7. _____

8. _____

9. _____

10. _____

B. Which aspects of God's positive parenting might be particularly helpful for you to develop with your children?

1. _____

2. _____

3. _____

4. _____

5. _____

Exercises for Chapter 2

Your Child *Is* Different!

No two children are totally alike. Based on their physical and mental endowments and their basic temperament styles, every child enters this world with his or her own unique personality. Some children are basically easy to parent. Some are slow to warm up. And others can be *very* difficult. Coupled with their position in the family, the quality of parent-child interaction, and the influence of the broader social environment—all of these factors work together to shape your child's unique personality.

This uniqueness can be a blessing or a curse to parents. Few experiences are more rewarding than watching the gradual unfolding of our children's unique abilities, gifts, and personalities. One is quiet and reflective. One is shy and reserved. One is a born social butterfly. And one rushes in "where angels fear to tread"! But the same individuality that entertains and rewards us can also be the bane of our existence. Just when we think we have learned to understand our

first one, a new one with a totally different style comes along!
Some of us also have one child who seems to be a problem no
matter what we try. These "difficult children" have a thousand ways of worrying us and making us feel like failures!

In chapter 2 we looked at several reasons no two children
are totally alike. In this chapter we will look at our own personalities as well as our children's so we can see what causes
some children to be so different.

Exercise 1

If you are using this material in a class or study group, divide
yourselves into smaller groups on the basis of your own birth
order. Put all "only children" in one group, all "first children"
in another, all "youngest children" in another, and all "sandwich children" in another. If you are doing this exercise as a
couple or as an individual, think back on your own childhood
experiences, especially your understanding of yourself in relation to your siblings, and complete parts A and B.

A. Spend five or ten minutes discussing what it was like be-
    ing the only child, the sandwich child, or whatever other
    place you had in your family. Then list several advantages
    and disadvantages of being in your particular spot in the
    family.

    Advantages of being first (middle, last, etc.) child.

    1. _____

    2. _____

    3. _____

    4. _____

Disadvantages of being first (middle, last, etc.) child.

1. _____

2. _____

3. _____

4. _____

B. Now list some of the personality characteristics the majority of your group members seem to have in common. Since many things influence our personalities, there will be a lot of variation, but you may see some patterns. Do members of your group, for example, tend to be aggressive, dependent, passive, achievement oriented, cooperative, competitive, leaders, followers, outgoing, quiet, etc.? And do they have large families, college educations, professional positions, etc.?_____

_____

_____

_____

C. Now share the characteristics, advantages, and disadvantages with members of other groups and notice the similarities and differences among the personalities of people with different positions in the family. List some of the differences below.

_____

_____

_____

_____

D. Do your experiences or those of your friends shed any

light on the personalities of any of your children? If so, how?_____

_____

_____

Exercise 2

A. Contrast at least four of the main personality characteristics, aptitudes, and interests you had as a child or teenager with those of one of your brothers or sisters. In other words, how did you differ from one of your brothers or sisters? Choose a same-sexed sibling if possible.

1. _____
2. _____
3. _____
4. _____
5. _____

B. Did these differences make life easier, more difficult, or have no effect? _____ If they made life easier or more difficult for you than it was for your brother or sister, tell how. Be as detailed as possible and try to recall how you really *felt* about these differences as a child (e.g., proud, happy, discouraged, confused, jealous, resentful, appreciative etc.)._____

_____

_____

_____

C. Were your parents sensitive to the unique styles of you

and your siblings and able to adapt to your individual characteristics? If so, share how they did this below. If they did not, what effect did it have on you and your siblings?_____

_____

_____

_____

_____

_____

Exercise 3

Circle the words below that best describe each of your children. Use a different color pen for your eldest child, your youngest child, and any additional children.

quiet	reflective	aggressive
follower	outgoing	reserved
patient	loud	leader
unpredictable	rigid	insensitive
thoughtful	impulsive	active
moody	cheerful	consistent
studious	competitive	flexible

Exercise 4

Children with different personalities evoke different responses from parents.

A. Which of your children is the easiest for you to parent? Explain why. Also, how does this child make you feel?

_____

_____

_____

_____

_____

B. Which of your children frustrates you most easily or is the most difficult to parent? Explain why. How does this child make you feel?_____

_____

_____

_____

_____

C. Where or how do you think your child developed the characteristics that "bug" you?_____

_____

_____

_____

D. What positive potential might be hidden under the very traits that frustrate you most about your difficult child?

_____

_____

_____

_____

E. How might you grow and change in order to be able to understand your difficult child and avoid making him or

her feel "odd," "bad," or "different"? In other words,
what do you need to be able to do to accept his or her
unique style or manner and channel it in a God-given
direction?_____

_____

_____

_____

_____

Exercises for Chapter 3

Mommy, Do You Love Me?

Many of our children's and teenagers' misbehaviors and problems grow out of their attempts to fulfill hidden needs for love, confidence, worth, and constructive activity by turning to substitutes of attention, power, perfectionism, and destructive activity. Although we love our children, we can so easily get caught up in vocational, educational, recreational, or spiritual activities that we unknowingly fail to communicate to them a deep sense of love and belonging. In chapter 3 we saw it was not enough to love our children—or even for them to intellectually "know" they are loved. If we are to instill a deep sense of love that will both fulfill our children's inner needs and minimize their tendency to misbehave in order to gain attention, we must learn to daily express our love in ways they can understand and appreciate.

This chapter is designed to help you think of practical, enjoyable ways of communicating your love to your children so that they will understand and believe it.

Exercise 1

Select a chapter from one of the Gospels (Matthew, Mark, Luke, or John) and read it, giving special attention to how Jesus communicated His love. (Suggestions: Matthew 9, 10, 14, 15, 18, 27, and many others from Mark, Luke, and John.)

A. List the ways below

    1. _____

    2. _____

    3. _____

    4. _____

    5. _____

B. How would you have felt if you had been on the receiving end of Jesus' love as described in this chapter?_____

_____

_____

_____

_____

_____

_____

_____

Exercise 2

Fill out the following chart with your husband or wife. Use different color pens so you can identify your own activities.

Think through the past week (or a "typical" week) one day at a time and fill in the amount of time you spent in each

	Work outside of home	Household chores	Time spent eating	Time in car	Watching TV	Phone	Church-related activities	Sleeping	Other	Individual time per child
Monday										
Tuesday										
Wednesday										
Thursday										
Friday										
Saturday										
Sunday										

activity listed on the chart. After you have filled out the first nine categories, fill in the one called "individual time per child" with the amount of time you spent in *meaningful* communication with each child daily. *Meaningful* does not mean watching television at the same time, a passing "Good morning. Have a good sleep?" or a brief, "Hi. How was your day?" Instead, it means laying other things aside and giving our full attention to our sons or daughters. We may do this over mealtime (if we are *really* communicating), while playing ball or doing yardwork *together*, or in many other ways. The key is that we really share of ourselves and take time to understand our children's thoughts, feelings, and activities.

Exercise 3

One of the best ways of understanding our children's needs and ways of meeting them is to place ourselves in our children's shoes. Think back over a three-year period of your life sometime between the ages of six and eighteen and complete the items below.

A. Discuss and list below your happiest times with and the times you felt most loved by your father._____

_____

_____

_____

_____

B. Discuss and list below your happiest times with and the times you felt most loved by your mother._____

_____

_____

_____

_____

C. Describe the positive feelings you felt in A and B as viv-
   idly as you can by using "live" words like *warm*, *close*,
   fulfilled, *peaceful*, *excited*, etc. Explain precisely how it made
   you feel to have these experiences with your parents.

_____

_____

_____

_____

D. Think back to times when you felt lonely, left out, isolated, or discouraged. What were your parents doing at
   these times? Why weren't you feeling loved, accepted,
   and encouraged?_____

_____

_____

_____

_____

E. What did you do or feel during the times you felt lonely or
   isolated? Be as detailed and specific as possible._____

_____

_____

_____

_____

F. What specific things do you wish your parents had done to help you feel more loved or a more important member of the family?_____

_____

_____

_____

Exercise 4

A. Based on your discussions in exercises 2 and 3, do you believe you are spending sufficient quality time daily with your children to help them develop a deep feeling of belonging and being loved? _____

If not, what specific things can you do that will help you communicate your love in ways your children can understand and accept?

1. _____

2. _____

3. _____

4. _____

5. _____

B. What otherwise good activities that are limiting your time with your children can you omit or cut down in order to spend more time with your children?

1. _____

2. _____

3. _____

4. _____

5. _____

Exercises for Chapter 4

Living in a World of Giants

Every human being has a God-given need for a sense of confidence. This confidence should ultimately be based on the fact that we are created and gifted by God. Unfortunately this sense of confidence is extremely fragile, especially in younger children. Criticism, overprotection, comparisons with siblings, and a host of other experiences can undermine a growing child's sense of confidence. When this happens, our children either give up and find psychological safety by losing their initiative or they struggle to compensate for feelings of inadequacy by fighting for power or control. This "power struggle" lies at the base of many family hassles.

Exercise 1

Darren and Rickie are brothers, ages eleven and ten. Darren is an argumentative, stubborn, know-it-all type child who gives his mother fits with his constant negativism. Rickie is a quiet, rather fearful child who lives in his books and has few friends.

A. Take a few minutes to discuss all of the possible experiences or *family dynamics* that may have caused these children to become the way they are. Then list those possibilities.

1. _____

2. _____

3. _____

4. _____

5. _____

6. _____

7. _____

B. Make a list of other possible reasons Darren and Rickie are so different, giving special attention to both boys' needs for confidence and their ways of handling those needs.

1. _____

2. _____

3. _____

4. _____

5. _____

6. _____

7. _____

C. Now assume Rickie and Darren were your children. What could you do to help each of them develop a greater sense of confidence? Be as specific as possible.

1. _____

2. _____

3. _____

4. _____

5. _____

6. _____

7. _____

Exercise 2

A. The Bible provides a strong foundation for a sense of confidence. It says we are created in God's image, gifted by God, redeemed by Christ, and indwelled by the Holy Spirit. One important way to help our children develop a healthy sense of confidence is to teach them what the Bible has to say about their abilities and importance to God. Discuss with your spouse or study group scriptural passages and concepts you can share with your children to help them develop a biblical sense of confidence, and list them below.

1. _____

2. _____

3. _____

4. _____

5. _____

6. _____

7. _____

B. Select one thing you have been doing that might make it difficult for one or more of your children to develop a healthy sense of confidence. Discuss this with your spouse or study group and write it out below. For the next week make a concentrated and prayerful effort to avoid this reaction. Next week share your success with your study group._____

_____

_____

_____

C. Select two or three specific ways to build up your children's sense of confidence. Discuss these with your spouse or study group and write them out below. For one week make a concentrated effort to *daily* help your children develop confidence by these reactions. Next week share your success with your study group._____

_____

_____

_____

Exercise 3

Most of our children have beautiful ways of sucking us into a power struggle. They "forget" to do their chores; they "don't hear"; or they bait us with comments like, "No! I won't."

A. Describe (or discuss with your study group) a recent power struggle between yourself and one of your children. Be as specific as possible._____

_____

_____

_____

_____

B. Think back over the power struggle you just described and answer the following questions:

1. How do you think your child was feeling when he or she tried to pull you into a power struggle (e.g., happy, sad, calm, tense, frustrated, confident, lonely, bored, etc.)?_____

   _____

   _____

2. How were you feeling at the time?_____

   _____

   _____

   _____

   _____

3. How did your child attempt to draw you into the struggle?_____

   _____

   _____

   _____

   _____

4. How do you think he or she expected you to respond?

   _____

   _____

   _____

5. Did you? _____

6. How could you have responded differently? In other words, what could you have said or done that would have showed that you understood your child's wishes and feelings and led to a resolution of the problem instead of another fight?_____

_____

_____

_____

_____

C. If you are in a study group, ask two or three members of the group to share a recent time when they started to be drawn into a power struggle but then saw it coming and found a way of sidestepping it. Discuss these situations and jot down any principles or ideas that might help you avoid similar situations._____

_____

_____

_____

_____

Exercises for Chapter 5

Is Your Child "Too Good"?

Some outwardly well-adjusted children actually may not feel good about themselves at all. For some reason they have failed to develop a healthy sense of worth or value as individuals. Consequently they are prone to feelings of depression, guilt, and self-depreciation, which they attempt to ward off through perfectionistic behavior.

Exercise 1

Cheryl is sixteen years old, the third of four children. Her father is a successful businessman and her mother is active in a number of church and civic organizations. Cheryl has received A's in every course she has taken in the past four years with one exception. When that happened, she came home in tears and was angry at the teacher who "ruined my record!" Cheryl is active in her church youth group as well as the high school band, a couple of clubs, and the cheerleading squad.

She is always active in some activity and rarely takes time to "just relax." She is also planning to take a part-time job at a local fast-food restaurant after school.

A. If you could get inside of Cheryl's mind, how do you think she might be feeling (e.g., peaceful, tense, relaxed, happy, sad, lovable, etc.)?_____

_____

_____

_____

_____

B. Discuss and list below as many things as you can think of that might account for the pressure Cheryl seems to keep herself under._____

_____

_____

_____

_____

_____

_____

C. If you were Cheryl's parents, how might you help her feel better about herself and learn to ease up on her perfectionistic behavior?_____

_____

_____

_____

_____

D. How would you handle her desire to take a part-time job?

_____

_____

_____

_____

E. What biblical principles might be helpful in assisting Cheryl to overcome her perfectionism? Give both the biblical principle and specific Scripture references.

_____

_____

_____

_____

_____

_____

Exercise 2

Sometimes it is difficult to understand precisely how our children are thinking and feeling about themselves. Underneath their outwardly "natural" or "normal" behavior they may have a variety of hidden feelings.

A. Try to place yourself in one of your children's shoes and write an essay on how you think he or she thinks and feels about himself or herself. Imagine you are writing this essay for an anonymous publication and that you want it to communicate as much emotion as possible. You might include topics like "The thing I like most (or least) about myself," "How I feel about my body," and "How I feel when I fail." It might help to close your eyes and picture yourself looking like your son or daughter, wearing his or her clothing, having yourself for a parent, having his or her friends, etc. Write your essay on a separate page (or pages) of paper, and then write out in the space below how you felt putting yourself in your child's shoes. Also mention new insights into your child's feelings or things you learned from your essay._____

_____

_____

_____

_____

_____

B. Identify one or two of the negative feelings or self-perceptions you realized your child has as you wrote your essay. Then discuss and list below ways of helping your child develop a better sense of worth in that area._____

_____

_____

_____

_____

_____

_____

_____

_____

Exercise 3

Sometimes it is difficult to tell the difference between a talented person who likes to do well and a perfectionistic person who is compensating for an inner feeling of inferiority or a lack of worth.

A. Discuss this problem with your spouse or study group and make a list of several ways you might tell the difference.

1. _____

2. _____

3. _____

4. _____

5. _____

6. _____

B. Give an example of a child who may be either a well-adjusted, inwardly happy, and competent person or a perfectionist who is trying to compensate for hidden feelings of inferiority. Then tell why you think this person is one or the other._____

_____

_____

_____

_____

_____

Exercises for Chapter 6

"I'm Bored!"

When our children's God-given need for constructive activity is not met, they tend to become bored and search for substitute activities that are frequently destructive or at least distracting. Rainy days, days when parents are especially busy, or days when nothing much is planned can provide fertile soil for boredom and its not-so-boring consequences!

Exercise 1

A. Describe the way one or more of your children behave when they are bored. Be as specific as possible and mention pet phrases they use, facial expressions, attitudes, etc._____

_____

_____

_____

_____

_____

B. When your children become bored and start behaving the way you just described for an hour or so, how do you usually respond?_____

_____

_____

_____

_____

C. Think through a typical week at your home one day at a time. Decide what days (and what time of day) your children seem to have plenty of constructive activities to keep them occupied. Then decide the days (or times of day) they tend to become bored and search out substitute, destructive activities._____

_____

_____

_____

_____

D. What specific things do you think account for the differences between their good times and their bad times?____

_____

_____

_____

_____

E. Sit down with your children and plan some constructive

activities for two or three of your children's typical "bad times." Then list the plans you have made below and help your children carry them out. After you have done them, share with your study group or describe below how things went._____

_____

_____

_____

_____

_____

_____

_____

Exercise 2

A. Make a list of several times when your children tend to interrupt or disturb your activities. Then discuss the situations and decide why they always choose to interrupt at *these* times. (Hint: It is usually boredom or the search for attention.)

_____

_____

_____

_____

_____

_____

B. How do you typically respond to the interruptions you mentioned above? Specifically, have you been responding in ways that address the real problem—your children's boredom or need for a sense of love and belonging? Or have you missed these needs?_____

_____

_____

_____

_____

_____

C. What specific steps could you take that would either prevent these disruptions or handle them constructively?

1. _____
2. _____
3. _____
4. _____

Exercise 3

A. Think about a recent time you felt bored or disinterested in something, then describe that situation and your feelings at the time._____

_____

_____

_____

_____

B. How did you feel about your spouse and children and others close to you at that time?_____

_____

_____

_____

_____

C. List several things that can help you get out of a mood like that.

1. _____
2. _____
3. _____
4. _____

Exercises for Chapter 7

When Hidden Needs Aren't Met

In chapter 7 we saw that in addition to turning to substitutes for love, confidence, worth, and constructive activity, our children also develop problems out of a search for revenge and/or psychological safety. When their God-given needs are not met, they try to get even with us for not helping them meet their needs or they may turn to any of several defense mechanisms designed to help them avoid feeling unloved, incompetent, unworthy, or bored.

Exercise 1

First Samuel 18:6–12 tells an interesting story of the relationship between Saul, the king of Israel, and David.

> When the men were returning home after David
> had killed the Philistine, the women came out from
> all the towns of Israel to meet King Saul with sing-

ing and dancing, with joyful songs and with tambourines and lutes. As they danced, they sang:

"Saul has slain his thousands,
    and David his tens of thousands."

Saul was very angry; this refrain galled him. "They have credited David with tens of thousands," he thought, "but me with only thousands. What more can he get but the kingdom?" And from that time on Saul kept a jealous eye on David.

The next day an evil spirit from God came forcefully upon Saul. He was prophesying in his house, while David was playing the harp, as he usually did. Saul had a spear in his hand and he hurled it, saying to himself, "I'll pin David to the wall." But David eluded him twice.

Saul was afraid of David, because the Lord was with David but had left Saul.

A. Given the context of this story, why do you think Saul tried to kill David?_____

_____

_____

_____

B. Do you see either a search for revenge or psychological safety operating in this story? _____ Explain your answer._____

_____

_____

_____

_____

_____

C. If you were Saul, would you have felt so threatened by
   David so as to need to eliminate him?_____
   Why or why not?_____

   _____

   _____

   _____

Exercise 2

Beth is a negativistic fifteen-year-old who is often sullen and
argues with her mother at the drop of a hat. She is constantly
criticizing and acts as if her mother "can't do anything right."

A. In light of the six reasons children misbehave we have
   discussed so far, what are several possible reasons Beth
   may be acting this way?

   1. _____

   2. _____

   3. _____

   4. _____

B. Do you think Beth may be trying to get revenge on her
   mother? _____ If so, what might the mother have been
   doing (or not doing) that has made Beth want to get even
   with her?

   1. _____

   2. _____

3. _____

4. _____

C. What other things might be behind Beth's bad attitudes?

1. _____

2. _____

3. _____

4. _____

D. What might Beth's parents need to do in order to get to the source of her negativism and help her work it out?

1. _____

2. _____

3. _____

4. _____

Exercise 3

A. Make a list of things you do to avoid feeling unloved, incompetent, unworthy, or bored. In other words, what are your mechanisms of psychological safety? Discuss these with your mate or study group and list them below. (Hints: withdraw, escape into work, overcompensate, etc.)

1. _____

2. _____

3. _____

4. _____

B. What (or who) can gradually help you give up your hiding

or your search for psychological safety, and how do they do it?_____

_____

_____

_____

_____

_____

C. Do you see your children using these or other mechanisms of psychological safety? If so, which ones?

1. _____
2. _____
3. _____
4. _____

D. How can you sensitively help them through these difficult times?_____

_____

_____

_____

_____

_____

Exercises for Chapter 8

Isn't Anything Normal?

Not all of our children's misbehaviors stem from unmet needs for love, confidence, worth, or constructive activity. In fact, some of the most troubling problems we face as parents are *not* caused by these dynamics. Instead, they are simply normal human reactions that need to be dealt with by sensitive understanding and good training. The goal of this chapter is to learn to tell when "misbehavior" is a normal (and perhaps even healthy) reaction and when it points to unmet needs for love, confidence, worth, or constructive activity.

Exercise 1

A. Discuss with your spouse or study group which of the following "problems" are likely to be simply normal developmental reactions and which are likely to signal a search for attention, power, perfectionism, or destructive activity based on unmet emotional needs.

1. A sixteen-year-old boy who "refuses"   _____
   to clean his room.

2. An eight-year-old who is constantly   _____
   fighting.

3. A child who doesn't like to eat peas.   _____

4. A teenage girl who idolizes a current   _____
   movie star.

5. A teenage girl who "falls in love"   _____
   with every boy she dates.

6. A baby who kicks and screams while   _____
   his diaper is being changed.

7. A child who forgets to brush his teeth. _____

8. A teenager who is always snooping in   _____
   her sister's (or brother's or parents')
   possessions.

9. A toddler who gets into everything in   _____
   sight.

B. Each of the following "problems" could be either a normal
developmental reaction or the result of a search for attention, power, perfectionism, destructive activity, revenge,
or psychological safety. Discuss each situation with your
spouse or study group and decide under what conditions
each reaction would be normal and under what conditions
it could be caused by unmet needs.

1. A teenager who plays loudly whatever popular music is
   the current fad._____

   _____

_____

_____

_____

_____

_____

2. A boy who "doesn't like girls."_____

_____

_____

_____

_____

3. A teenage girl who seems to be in competition with her
   mother or who periodically criticizes and puts her
   mother down._____

_____

_____

_____

_____

4. A teenage boy who faithfully puts in at least one or two
   hours daily on weight lifting or other bodybuilding ex-
   ercises._____

_____

_____

_____

_____

_____

_____

5. A ten-year-old with a messy room._____

_____

_____

_____

_____

6. Siblings who fight a lot._____

_____

_____

_____

_____

7. A straight-A student._____

_____

_____

_____

_____

8. A child who "forgets" to do his/her chores._____

_____

_____

_____

_____

_____

Exercise 2

A. Select one problem reaction of each of your children, discuss it with your spouse or study group, and decide whether it is simply a normal reaction or if it also reflects a search to fulfill some unmet needs. Also tell how you arrived at your conclusion.

First Child's Problem Reaction_____

_____

_____

_____

_____

Second Child's Problem Reaction_____

_____

_____

_____

_____

Third Child's Problem Reaction_____

_____

_____

_____

_____

Fourth Child's Problem Reaction_____

_____

_____

_____

_____

B. Discuss one of the problem reactions above and decide
   how you might work differently with your child depending
   on whether it is simply a normal developmental reaction or
   an expression of some unmet need. Discuss this with your
   spouse or study group and be as specific as possible._____

_____

_____

_____

_____

_____

_____

_____

Exercise 3

A. Select two biblical characters and discuss with your spouse
   or study group to what extent some of their problems
   might have been caused by unmet emotional needs. Then
   write out your conclusions and reasons for them below.
   (Possible examples, Adam and Eve, Isaac, David, Peter.)

_____

_____

_____

_____

_____

_____

_____

_____

B. What can we learn from these biblical examples?_____

_____

_____

_____

_____

_____

Exercises for Chapter 9

Your Child and Adam

In chapter 9 we looked at the role sin plays in our children's problems or misbehaviors. In the exercises in this chapter we will review those concepts and apply our understanding to some practical situations in our own families.

Exercise 1

A. List the two ways sin is involved in the development of our children's misbehaviors.

1. _____

2. _____

B. Read the brief description below and answer questions 1–3.

Jim and John are both eleven years of age and each also has a nine-year-old sister with whom he is often fighting.

Jim's father is a workaholic who takes little time to relax and enjoy life with his family, and his mother is usually busy with church activities or with his younger sister. John's dad, although he holds a management position, takes some time each day to be with John and his sister. They also do a lot of family things together.

1. Which boy's parents are more likely to be contributing to their son's fighting? _____ Why? _____

   _____

   _____

   _____

2. Which boy probably is more directly responsible for his own fighting? _____ Why? _____

   _____

   _____

   _____

3. Do you think these parents might need to help Jim and John with their fighting in different ways? _____ If so, how? (Be specific.) _____

   _____

   _____

   _____

Exercise 2

A. Select two of your own problems or negative traits, discuss them briefly with your spouse or study group, and describe them below._____

_____

_____

_____

B. Do you see ways in which your parents contributed to your negative traits? _____ If so, how? _____

_____

_____

_____

C. Do you see ways you needed to be "number one" or ways you contributed to your own problem reaction? _____ If so, how? _____

_____

_____

_____

(If you have trouble answering these, ask your spouse to help you. I am sure he or she will be able to point out a few things!)

D. What could your parents have done that might have helped you overcome or minimize your negative traits?

1. _____

2. _____

3. _____

4. _____

5. _____

Exercise 3

Pick a problem or a misbehavior of one of your children, discuss it with your spouse or study group, and complete the section below.

A. Describe the problem._____

_____

_____

_____

B. Do you see ways you have been contributing to the problem by not sufficiently helping your child meet his/her needs for love, confidence, worth, and constructive activities? _____ If so, how?_____

_____

_____

_____

C. Do you see other ways you have contributed to the problem? _____ If so, how? _____

_____

_____

_____

D. Do you see ways your child's own sinful tendencies add to the problem? _____ If so, what are they?_____

_____

_____

_____

E. What could you do to take your part in solving the problem?_____

_____

_____

_____

_____

F. What could your child do to help work it out?_____

_____

_____

_____

_____

_____

Exercises for Chapter 10

Finding Your Child's Hidden Needs

Chapter 10 summarizes the reasons why our children tend to misbehave and shows how we can tell which one or two of these causes are behind any particular problems. We do that by looking at (1) our childrens' behaviors, (2) our reactions and feelings, and (3) our childrens' reactions to our discipline. These exercises help you practice finding the hidden needs behind your childrens' problems.

Exercise 1

Summarize the seven reasons children misbehave and describe how the process works by giving an illustration of a typical misbehavior of one of your children. (Be as detailed as possible about how your child's misbehavior functions and the role you may be playing in it.)_____

_____

_____

_____

_____

_____

_____

_____

_____

_____

_____

_____

_____

_____

_____

Exercise 2

Discuss each of the following typical behaviors with your spouse or study group and fill in the motivation that is most likely causing the misbehavior. Give both the unmet God-given need and the substitute and also tell if there is a search for revenge or psychological safety. Remember that your child's behavior gives clues to his or her hidden needs. (If you need to review, see Table I on page 139.)

	Need	Substitute	Others
1. A very "good" child who is easily upset and discouraged when she doesn't do well			
2. A show-off			
3. A shy, withdrawn child			
4. A stubborn child			
5. Teenagers who get into trouble when they are "just cruising"			
6. A negativistic child who is always putting down his younger brother			

Exercise 3

One of the best ways of figuring out what is causing our children to misbehave is to monitor our reactions to our child. Which goal is probably motivating your child when you feel the following way:

	Need	Substitute	Others
1. You feel as if you are in a contest or a battle.			
2. You wish your child would stop interrupting you.			
3. You are really angry and want to "get even with that child."			
4. You just don't know how to reach this child.			
5. You wish your child would leave you alone and take care of himself.			
6. You feel proud of your child but are afraid she may "overdo it."			

Exercise 4

The final way of deciding which goal is motivating your child's misbehavior is to look at his/her response to discipline. Which reasons are probably promoting the following children to misbehave, if they respond to correction as follows?

	Need	Substitute	Others
1. He stops for a short time but then begins again.			
2. He gets worse when disciplined.			
3. He tries harder but feels criticized and feels as if he can never do well enough.			
4. He continues to argue, fight, or find some other way to get his way.			
5. He feels misunderstood or discouraged and may keep interrupting.			
6. He continues to be "hard to reach."			

Exercise 5

We can break down the process of helping our children grow out of their problems and misbehaviors into at least six steps.

The first step is to identify the specific problem we want to work on. It is usually better to select a specific problem like being late, sassiness, messy rooms, or sibling fights, than a vague or general problem like "Our home is in chaos from morning till night!" It is also best to work on only one or two problems at a time.

After we select the problem we want to work on, we need to decide which (if any) unmet needs and what substitute goals are influencing the misbehavior. We also need to decide if the misbehavior reflects a search for revenge or psychological safety or a normal developmental reaction.

The third step is to help our children understand the causes of their misbehavior and help them find better ways of communicating their needs for love, confidence, worth, and constructive activity or their desires for revenge or psychological safety.

At the same time, we need to see that we are not unknowingly rewarding their substitute goals by giving them the attention, power, or other things they are looking for through their misbehaviors.

A fifth step is to back up and see what we can do to more fully meet our children's needs so they will be less inclined to misbehave to find substitutes for their God-given needs.

These first five steps are all part of positive parenting. They are ways of understanding our children and helping meet their needs before they develop serious problems. They are also the first steps in resolving common misbehaviors. To tie all of this together, pick one or more of your child's problems or misbehaviors and complete the steps below:

A. State the problem clearly and in as much detail as possible._____

_____

_____

_____

_____

_____

B. Which one or two of the seven reasons for misbehaviors seem to be operating most strongly in this situation?

_____

_____

_____

_____

C. The next time your child acts this way take time to listen
carefully to what he/she must be feeling and help him/her
understand the God-given needs he/she may be trying to
fill in a negative way. Write out how he/she responded.

_____

_____

_____

_____

_____

D. What can you do to make sure you no longer reward your
child's misbehavior by seeing that you don't simply give
him the attention, power, etc., that he wants for the misbehavior?_____

_____

_____

_____

_____

_____

E. Make a list of specific things you will do to meet your
child's basic need in order to lessen his search for substitutes.

1. _____

2. _____

3. _____

4. _____

5. _____

The final step in effective child rearing and problem solving is corrective discipline. The five steps we have covered in this book will go a long way toward resolving problems but all children will still need a good bit of corrective discipline.

Since this book is aimed largely at prevention, we have not gone into detail on what to do after your children misbehave. My book *Help! I'm a Parent* is written for that purpose. It begins at the point this book leaves off. Identifying your children's hidden needs is the foundation of good parenting but even when you meet your children's needs they will sometimes misbehave and need correction. *Help! I'm a Parent* addresses five specific methods of discipline and shows how to apply those methods to daily problems like messy rooms, sibling fights, mealtime and homework hassles, temper tantrums, curfew violations, and other family problems. These two books are written to be used together—*Your Child's Hidden Needs* to understand your children's needs and how you can more effectively fulfill them in order to avoid as much misbehavior as possible—and *Help! I'm a Parent* to see what you can do after your children misbehave. Best wishes for a sane, successful, and enjoyable experience of parenting!